OTHER BOOKS BY JOHN F. WASIK

The Late-Start Investor

The Investment Club Book

Green Marketing and Management: A Global Perspective

Retire Early

—and Live the Life You Want Now

JOHN F. WASIK

Retire Early

—and Live the Life You Want Now

**A 10-Step Plan for
Reinventing Your Retirement**

Henry Holt and Company ▪ New York

Henry Holt and Company, LLC
Publishers since 1866
115 West 18th Street
New York, New York 10011

Henry Holt® is a registered trademark of
Henry Holt and Company, LLC.

Published in Canada by Fitzhenry & Whiteside Ltd.,
195 Allstate Parkway, Markham, Ontario L3R 4T8.

Library of Congress Cataloging-in-Publication Data

Wasik, John F.
Retire early—and live the life you want now :
a 10-step plan for reinventing your retirement /
John F. Wasik.—1st ed.
p. cm.
Includes bibliographical references and index.
ISBN 0-8050-6348-X (hb)
1. Retirement income. 2. Early retirement. 3. Retirement—Planning. I. Title.
HG179.W3194   2000
332.024'01—dc21   99-045391

Henry Holt books are available for special promotions and premiums.
For details contact: Director, Special Markets.

First Edition 2000

Designed by Jessica Shatan

Printed in the United States of America

10 9 8 7 6 5 4 3 2 1

CONTENTS

Step 8 ▪ 139

Making Your Money Last as Long as You Do

Techniques and vehicles for insulating and sustaining your new prosperity portfolio, including "safe" withdrawal methods, cash vehicles, buying the right kind of insurance, and choosing financial professionals.

Step 9 ▪ 160

Finding a Full Life after Leaving Full-Time Work Behind

Making the transition to your new prosperity, including a focus on easing out of full-time work; relationships; spirituality; religion; charity; and other concerns.

Step 10 ▪ 181

Putting It All Together and Launching
Your Personal Pursuit of Happiness

The final details of your new prosperity plan, highlighting your commitment to family, community, and others.

References ▪ 193

Resources ▪ 201

Index ▪ 211

PREFACE

The universe constantly and obediently answers to our conceptions;
whether we travel fast or slow, the track is laid for us. Let us spend our
lives in conceiving them.
                                        —Henry David Thoreau, *Walden*

A malaise haunts our Western culture at the end of the machine
age. It is the feeling that despite all of our successful careers, opportunities, advanced health care, longer lifespans, and prosperity, we
never get to do what we want to do in life. The cycle of work,
leisure, and daily activity is wearing us down to a nub. Our immediate response is to pose the philosophical statement: "If I won the
lottery, I would . . ." Well of course you would, but you probably
won't win the lottery.

There is clearly another path that is more satisfying than the one
we know. We yearn for it every day of our working lives. It involves
a recognition that there are several sides to our "selves," although
those different faces are often hidden by the demands of industrial
age society. That's why for most of us, it's hard to break the chains
that make us wage slaves. Many of us feel that we are doomed to
work at a job we despise until we drop. But as Carl Jung proposed
in his theory of individuation, we all subscribe to a personal myth
about ourselves and our families. We may believe we are homely,

stupid, or just bad at math. We may believe that we deserve better, should drive a sports car, or have a perfect body. Or we may want to hide from ourselves because our parents told us we would never amount to anything. How you choose to live reflects what you believe and the vision you have of yourself—often shaded by what others say we are. We all create a mythology for ourselves, which often impairs our ability to let our inner selves truly live. From the little storm clouds that drift into our dissatisfied minds at the end of the day, we hear the thunderclap refrain, "Is that *all* there is to my life?" Fortunately, we can reshape our futures by creating a new, passionate mythology based on a healthy relationship (or ecology) with ourselves, our livelihoods, our money, and our dreams.

This book is about creating a positive, prosperous, and passionate new vision for ourselves and making it come true by actively pursuing it. I term this new form of self-regard a "new prosperity." This new way of living is often linked with a retirement, although it's really about a *sustainable* life that balances some work with leisure, family, and community activities more than it is about leaving a job. In many ways, this new prosperity is what you might call an early retirement, in that you won't have to work as hard or as long and you will certainly reap more time for the life you've only dreamed of living until now. Prosperity is traditionally associated with success and wealth, but its extended definition includes a vigor, a life force. One of the Latin roots of prosperity, is *spes*, which means hope. The monetary side of wealth—cash, stocks, bonds, mutual funds, real estate—is cold, nonliving. The human side of wealth is prosperity, a living entity that needs to be nourished, nurtured, educated, probed, cherished, and understood. A new prosperity, in short, is a deeply meaningful relationship between life, work, and money, a personal ecology that encompasses definitions of work, leisure, family, spirituality, and community.

Finding a new prosperity is a matter of balancing our aspirations with our failures, our spending with our savings, and our hopes with our abilities. In balancing our lives for early retirement, we discover other dynamic lives within us, like turning over a log in a forest and finding life in hundreds of forms, teeming, recycling, and growing.

What This Book Will Do for You
(and How to Best Use It)

This is not a book that you *have* to start with the first chapter and read all the way to the end. After all, everyone's in a different place in life. The chapters provide the most comprehensive way of looking at a number of life issues, so you can choose where you need to be and start with the chapter that sets you on your journey.

If you are looking for a get-rich-quick book, keep in mind I have no secret formulas for playing the stock market, day-trading on the Internet, or buying real estate with no money down. I do, however, share several consistently profitable methods of investing that work for millions. I won't tell you how to become a Buddhist, climb a mountain in a Third World country, or quote Sufi poetry, although those things are perfectly fine and are covered quite well in other books. Nor is this a "recovery" book, a "financial diet" book, or a book that asks you to peer at your navel while contemplating retirement nirvana. This book will, however, help you find a healthy relationship with the money you've earned in the workforce and tell you about the powerful activities you should consider as you build an early-retirement plan.

Since I'm primarily an investigative journalist and teacher, I've culled the knowledge and wisdom of some of the best financial minds in the country as I gathered the material for this book. I've also researched the best texts, the best online resources, and found some interesting people to talk about how they see their new prosperity. So here's how to use this book to craft a new prosperity plan:

If you are befuddled about your entire financial picture . . . please start with Step 1 and work your way through. This book gets progressively more advanced in financial planning details. Step 2 looks at your expense/income "portrait" and helps you answer questions about what you need to do to plan, save, invest, and sustain your life-income portfolio. Once you have a good idea where to begin in terms of savings, spending, and income alignment, work through the book toward the end. Step 3 will give you some ideas on how much you need to save to retire, how to create an income stream, and some other important considerations. Steps 4, 6, 7, and 8 will provide strategies on how to fund and maintain your portfolios. Every step is designed to give you one more tool to help you build a new prosperity plan and fund your new prosperity portfolio.

Although I provide ten steps to reinvent your retirement, you may not need to study each one, especially if you are further along on the investing side, facing a corporate buyout, or are in a position to draw upon a steady income stream for the rest of your life without a full-time job. Within the ten steps are many suggestions and exercises on how to do the essential balancing between income, expenses, family, self, and community. No matter where you are on your road to new prosperity, it would be helpful to review each chapter as you give yourself a status report on the fundamentals of your early retirement plan. Here are some shortcuts:

If you have a reasonably complete picture of how much you earn and spend . . . jump to step 3, where I discuss a number of early retirement planning strategies. You may, however, want to backtrack a bit to complete the income/spending worksheets in step 2 to make some choices about how to achieve a new prosperity. You may not need the information in step 4 if you are fully funding your retirement vehicles, but you will definitely need to read step 8 on maintaining and insulating your life income for a lengthy retirement. Step 10, the last chapter, gives you a jump start on your new prosperity plan, and the summation will be helpful to all readers.

If you've done all your financial homework and know you have the money to leave the workforce soon . . . then browse steps 2 and 3 and head right into steps 5, 9, and 10. These steps provide insights into your life and show you how to create a fulfilling early-retirement plan once you have all of the financial details sorted out.

This book is designed as a guidebook to *your* life. You fill in the itinerary. With no right or wrong path, every step you take is the beginning of a thrilling new adventure. Time will be in short supply and money in heavy demand—you'll benefit greatly if you know how to navigate. The road we travel is snow-laden and slick, our journey challenging and quick. So enjoy the ride while you can.

I hope this book will be a tool you use to guide you through life's challenges, and that it will add to the insight and information you need to live the life you've only dreamed of until now.

ACKNOWLEDGMENTS

This book owes its inception to the scintillating leadership of John Sterling and the divine stewardship of Amelia Sheldon, my partners at Henry Holt and Company. My agent, Robert Shepard, lent more than his wisdom and expertise—his kindness and loyalty are incomparable.

Stephanie and Gordon Medlock—and everyone at the John Joseph Group—were more than helpful. They introduced me to the Mussmans and Margaret Huyck, who were all beyond gracious with their time. Donald Kraft, Dick Parker, Marsha McBroom, and John Greaney were instrumental in showing me the mechanics of early retirement. My researcher, Michelle Schwartz, always came through in a pinch.

My friends in financial planning were first-rate in their insights and advice: Jim Platania, Mike Leonetti, and Sue Stevens. For spiritual guidance, I have to thank Pat Gaughan, Frank Butler, Father Tom Enright, and Father Bob Aguirre.

Enduring my peskiness on a daily basis is no easy task. For that I'd like to thank my employers at *Consumers Digest*, Art and Randy Weber, and my patient editor-in-chief, John Manos. My friends and colleagues Jim Gorzelany, Beverly Sherman, Nicole Hopewell, Carey Millsap-Spears, and everyone else at *Consumers Digest* are deserving of my utmost gratitude.

To all of my Forest Garden neighbors, particularly Vicki and Ralph, Fred and Esther, Nikki and Al, Darcy, Lenny and Josh, and Jan and Bruce—Kathleen and I grew wiser being among you.

None of this would have been possible, however, without the support, forbearance, and love of my family (the Wasiks—Tom, TJ, Annie—and the Conlons, McGoverns, and Flemings) and, most of all, my celestial muses Kathleen Rose and Sarah Virginia; and especially my father, Arthur, and my mother, Virginia.

Retire Early

—and Live the Life You Want Now

Focusing on How *Your* Retirement Will Be Different

Whatever you can do, or dream you can do, begin it. Boldness has genius, power, and magic in it.

—Johann Wolfgang von Goethe

It's easy to say, "Okay, when we *have* the money we'll leave everything behind and spend our remaining hours on the beach drinking away the small moments and soaking up the sun." That is the persistent image of what has become *retirement,* the ultimate playground of our later years, when work ceases and we typically occupy ourselves solely with leisure pursuits. This conventional model of retreat from work may be possible for some of us. But why wait until sixty-two or sixty-five to pursue it if you don't have to? Why wait for a company to pony up the necessary salary and benefits in a job market that's more volatile every year? The new rules of retirement say that the new prosperity of early retirement can be yours in your thirties, forties, and fifties if you plan right.

A number of reasons tell us why a new prosperity is possible. We're living longer. The fastest-growing demographic group today is one-hundred-year-olds. We're able to maintain health and stave off once-fatal diseases. Our kids may still live at home and we're having them later in life. Our parents are living longer and we may need to take care of them even while we're still attending to our children's needs. As a result of this cornucopia of longevity, we have options our grandparents never had: a second or third career; a chance to integrate less work with more leisure; a new life that breaks all the old rules. Combine that with a golden era of retirement vehicles—401(k)s, 403(b)s, IRAs, etc.—and you may have the means to jump off the lumbering cattle car of the 40-hour workweek much earlier than age sixty-five, an arbitrary retirement age if there ever was one.

There's a growing demand and restlessness among those who know that there's a better life they can start living before they hit sixty-five. More than half the people surveyed in a poll by Strong Funds, for example, said they wanted to retire before sixty-five; more than 60 percent said they would consider part-time work as a form of retirement.

The old paradigm of working thirty or forty years for the same company may be as extinct as the eight-track cassette player. Many Americans, bolstered by one of the most vibrant stock markets in years, may be able to leave the workforce after less than twenty years. By my estimate, there may be as many as twenty million American workers who will be in a financial position to leave the full-time workforce in the next five years. That's good news if you're in that boat; if you're not, you can do some "prosperity planning" to get there, which is what this book is all about. If low inflation continues and increased productivity from technology continues to lower corporate operating costs—and boost earnings—your prosperity portfolio will keep on growing.

There is no magic formula to make your work life disappear. There are, however, a number of observations, formulas, and course corrections you can make to balance your everyday activities with those you've only dreamed of until now. These formulas—explored in subsequent chapters—add up to a whole of a life well-lived. But

SOURCES OF RETIREMENT INCOME*

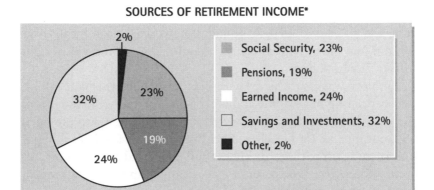

Social Security, 23%

Pensions, 19%

Earned Income, 24%

Savings and Investments, 32%

Other, 2%

Source: U.S. Department of the Treasury, 1993
*For households with retirement income over $20,000 a year.

before we do the math on the details of your daily grind, we need to explore some obstacles that may be standing in your way and how we can overcome them. It's possible to have a revelation of what your new prosperity could be—when you least expect it.

My Own New Prosperity Revelation

One recent gray April I found myself wondering what I had done to deserve the downpour of bad luck that had fallen upon myself and my family. I was treading water in one of those inexorable monsoons of life and feared I was spiritually drowning. I was thinking seriously of leaving journalism after nearly twenty years; for what, I didn't know. It didn't seem as though I was writing stories that were challenging me or reaching people the way I wanted them to. Until now I had always felt called to the craft. So I was scared and depressed that writing wasn't getting me up in the morning. I might as well have been digging holes. Moreover, my commute was up to four hours a day in bad weather and our house was still a wreck after six years of remodeling. Sections were covered with house wrap as my wife, Kathleen, and I saved the money to re-side it. I suddenly wondered why we were sinking so much money into a house, even if it was on a beautiful lot. It was too far from civilization and the hundred-mile round trip to work in Chicago was wearing me out. I had no energy to enjoy the natural world right outside my back door.

Kathleen was also afflicted with the melancholia that comes with deconstructing one's home and life. She wanted to walk away from her software company, even though it was successful and provided a decent income for herself and her brother. Constantly building it and keeping up with needy clients had exhausted her. In short, we were the perfect postmodern American couple: having much, wanting more, getting less. In addition to that angst, my father-in-law, Joe, was undergoing a heart procedure to correct an anomaly. Kathleen was at the hospital with her mother, Theresa, to await word on his surgery on that pallid April afternoon.

There was only one thing I wanted to do as I awaited word on Joe: go for a walk. I took our two German shepherds, Marco and Ella, to the farm field behind my house. What called me to the field wasn't so much a relief from the stress of the day, but the trumpeting of sandhill cranes, the majestic long-winged, red-capped birds that stopped by during their migration from Florida to Wisconsin. I had heard them before. They beckoned to me like sirens, only not calling me to rocky shoals but to a prehistoric dance I was yet to witness fully. For forty million years, these birds have been migrating without so much as a satellite system to get them from the subtropics to the northern woods. There was a reason that the mythology of every ancient culture from the Egyptian to the Japanese depicted them as harbingers of fertility and luck. Devoted for life, breeding pairs stay together during every migration, signaling to each other with their unearthly clarion call which can be heard for miles. What was the intimate relationship between these traveling cranes and the disappearing wetlands of northern Illinois? My little expedition harkened back my passionate interest in natural philosophy and ecology, something I would gladly take up full-time or even part-time if it could pay the mortgage, the car payments, and finish our endless renovations. At least for now, however, I was resigned to the role of gentleman naturalist, the

Darwin of a water-logged exurbia who could only spend moments each month out in the natural world I loved. This gentle prospect of *another life* triggered something in me that soggy day. I realized that there was life beyond my livelihood and that maybe I should start planning for it holistically—a strategy not focused on quitting work entirely but trimming back the hours a bit and making room to explore the other parts of my being.

What I discovered during that period was that I needed a new way of seeing life—one that would balance the work I needed to do and the "other life" I wanted. This passion would be an odyssey in and of itself, one that would incite and excite, exercise and exorcise, construct and deconstruct the way we were reworking our home and life. In my case, the cranes were merely messengers to this new phase. Like Virgil in Dante's realm, they would guide me to new levels of purgatory and paradise. Journalism, writing, and teaching were fine, but they were work. What I needed was a way to pursue my true passions—and the means to finance my dream.

Several days after our darkest, wettest, and most put-upon month, a crane alighted on our front lawn, a mythic sign of good luck if ever there was one. A new life and an undefinable joy was upon us in more ways than one. A few weeks after this day, we found out we were pregnant and later welcomed our blue-eyed Sarah Virginia into the world, who has been beyond delightful to this day.

Just as I encountered rarities like cranes and coyotes in the middle of the industrial heartland, it's possible for you to have revelations of your own. You can build any future you want if you let yourself grow, have faith in your dreams or visions, and become open to new ideas. A new prosperity can be yours if you know where to look and how to plan. First, however, you'll need to deconstruct the conventional wisdom and barriers that are preventing you from considering an early retirement.

Barriers and Bromides: What's Keeping Us from an Early Retirement?

It's clear that the post–World War II generation may not want to work as long as their parents did, but what will replace that monolithic "work-until-65 model?" Consider this observation: "The baby boomers have yet to achieve a consensus as to what the nature of work, careers, retirement, or the work-family interface should be. Yet, given the changes in the macroeconomy, work, longevity, retirement, families, gender roles, and the labor force, current assumptions and practices seem increasingly outmoded and inappropriate." This analysis, as presented in the research report "The Future of Work and Retirement Needs: Baby Boomers Express Their Views," suggests that over the next twenty years the whole concept of retirement will undergo unprecedented changes.

Although that last statement refers to baby boomers, the three generations who follow them are also looking to fashion a nonstandard retirement. To understand the competing elements of our lives, which we must consider as we explore the question of early retirement, we need to probe the changing nature of work itself.

The world of work has gotten more complicated in the last half of the twentieth century. So to balance work with the rest of our lives in the twenty-first, we need to know what's happened and where we're going. The most important observation about work is that it's highly *fluid*. Careers come and go, corporations restructure, merge, and purge. We're bought out, downsized, and moved out at rates that would seem shocking in the staid 1950s when every worker was expected to remain loyal to one employer until retirement. Here's the reality check:

- The 1990s marked a record period of corporate changes, including more than 570,000 layoffs in 1998 alone, the largest number of job cuts in a decade according to the outplacement firm Challenger, Gray, and Christmas. Job security may be the most outmoded labor concept of our times.

- According the *Wall Street Journal*, "Americans have been retiring progressively earlier for about a century." Pension plans have allowed more participation in growth investments like stocks, workers have learned to better invest their money, and the stock market has been on a bull run for more than a decade.

- Some 90 million jobs out of a labor force of 124 million are "vulnerable to elimination" due to automation, according to social critic Jeremy Rifkin. No wonder only 51 percent of America's nonmanagement employees feel their jobs are secure—down from 75 percent ten years ago, Rifkin notes.

- There may be even bigger job jolts ahead as the global economy absorbs "the surging output of some 1.2 billion Chinese—more than one-fifth of the world's six billion people," according to economist Robert Reich.

- Not only do we have less job security, most of us have less control over the jobs we have. Union representation—and its protective collective bargaining—only accounts for less than 16 percent of the nonagricultural American workforce, according to *The Economist.*

- Combined with relatively low personal savings, the dislocations in the economy are making a conventional retirement less likely for millions who haven't saved or invested in the stock market. About one-third of baby boomers expect to "scale back their lifestyle during retirement," according to a survey by the American Association of Retired Persons (AARP). Moreover, eight out of ten baby boomers surveyed say they plan to work "at least part time during retirement," the survey found.

- All told, only some 20 to 25 percent of Americans surveyed by the Employment Benefit Research Institute (EBRI) feel confident they will have enough money to retire on comfortably.

- Since almost everybody seems to be living longer, we'll be able to leave the workforce early, start new careers, and pursue what sociologists call "a second adolescence." How important is the longevity factor? "*Global* life expectancy hit a new high of 66 years in 1998. A person born today will live 20 years—43 percent— longer than a person born at midcentury," according to the Worldwatch Institute. We need to plan for early retirement with the assumption that we will be around for a long period of time.

A New Prosperity Offers Hope for the Life You Want Now

Fortunately, we live in the golden era of retirement vehicles. There have never been more ways of obtaining a new prosperity before you hit your sixth decade. A select group of relatively simple strategies and investment vehicles can allow you to have a truly flexible new prosperity and leave the workforce when you want. That's the essence of steps 2, 4, 6, and 8.

The excuses we often recite that prevent us from enjoying a fruitful and timely retirement are ubiquitous: "I don't have enough money," "I still have kids or family members to support," "I can't save enough because every dollar goes out the door." Those barriers are also conquerable, and I'll give you specific strategies to do so in steps 2, 3, and 7. As the next step will illustrate (also see step 7 if you still have kids at home), there are hundreds of ways to change spending—and boost your income. The world is too much with us, Wordsworth once said, and we are working too hard to keep up with it, but there's no reason why we can't keep pace with the needs of our own lives. With the new goal of early retirement in mind, we have a strong new reason to adjust spending and saving and rebalance how we spend the precious time in our lives. I call this balancing act our personal ecology.

Finding a New Prosperity by Balancing Your Personal Ecology

Ecology is a beautiful word that is all about relationships. It shares the root word *oikos* with *economy,* which is from the classic Greek meaning household. A figurative translation is "keeping your house in order." Physicist Fritjof Capra has an even broader definition that calls ecology "the study of the relationships that interlink all members of the Earth Household." That lofty idea doesn't exclusively refer to the place in which you live, however. It refers to the life-energy you spend in working, commuting, relaxing, family time, playing, worshiping, or any other activity you can name. The relationships to these different "rooms" of our lives are interdependent. None can exist independently. We also need others in our lives. As Dr. Martin Luther King Jr. said, "All men [and women] are interdependent. Every nation is a vast treasury of ideas and labor to which both the living and the dead of all nations have contributed."

Personal ecology is about the relationships between all these activities and how they combine to make you a whole person. Perhaps you think you're not a whole person now or couldn't ever be one. Maybe some part of you was left behind in childhood or adolescence. While I believe that these essential parts of your personality can be revived and nurtured now or in the future, you still may *believe* that nothing will change because you have to work to make money to pay the bills. That's not the case.

Arriving at a sound personal ecology means a little *rebalancing* is in order. You may be able to make millions or billions of dollars in your lifetime and accumulate vast wealth, but unless you address the bigger picture of what else you do with your life—your total personal ecology—you'll never achieve *true prosperity*. Wealth that includes well-being is shared by you and your family, community and country, and that contributes to spiritual as well as material growth is true prosperity. It's like a prairie. In its original state, the prairie was an incredible biomechanical system that took sunlight and rain and converted it into biomass, the living matter that lived above and below the soil. Plants take nitrogen, carbon dioxide, and solar energy and convert it into oxygen, hundreds of species of grasses, forbs, and flowers, and fertile soil. Animals then benefit from what the prairie "produces." We harvest both the natives of the soil and the ruminants that graze on the plants. The chain of life continues as plants "share" their resources with animal life. As Richard Manning so elegantly describes in *Grassland* (Viking, 1995), "Through the solar-driven reaction of photosynthesis, plants use minerals provided by their roots, water from wherever they get it, atmospheric elements like nitrogen and carbon, mostly to form carbohydrates, which is energy, which is power, the driving force of all animal bodies, including ours."

I choose the metaphor of the prairie because I grew up around one south of Chicago and was entranced by its sensual power and organic prosperity—the flowing swishing of big bluestem, the rustling of Queen Anne's lace, the organic fragrance of a meadow after a thunderstorm. We have built much of modern American agriculture on the fertility of the midwestern prairie. We have also forgotten that this fertility can be easily depleted with overfarming, so we overapply fertilizers and pesticides and eventually end up poisoning our own water supplies, creating flooding and erosion problems where none existed for more than ten thousand years. In our own personal ecology, we can poison our own little ecosystems. We can spend too much money and life-energy on any number of things that will deplete our resources. As a result, we can be out of balance with the needs of our lives. You can restore your own life's prosperity, however, by observing a few tenets on the way to a new prosperity.

PRINCIPLES OF PERSONAL ECOLOGY

- **We can balance our lives.** The relationship between work, leisure, family life, and other activities can be harmonized.

- **Money can be used to propel our dreams.** Money has value, power, and the ability to transform our lives. Saving, spending, and earning power can be balanced according to our needs. A first step on this rebalancing route is to save more than we spend—preferably at least 10 percent of our annual income. You can retire early, but to do so you have to make money work efficiently for you. Saving and investing are the two important tools that will give you leverage in your new prosperity.

- **Work can be redefined and help us reach our goals.** We can achieve a total balance in our life by including different kinds of work, not by excluding work altogether. New prosperity doesn't eliminate work entirely, it refocuses our efforts toward different modes of work.

- **Personal growth will make much of the struggle easier.** Growth is possible and necessary for a long, prosperous life (see step 9). Given the volatile state of the global economy, you'll need some "re-employment insurance" (Robert Reich's term) to keep up with the changing demands of the workplace. What we don't know about the job market and the world at large can be learned through education, which is a lifelong process of mental, spiritual, and social enrichment and not a finite collection of degrees.

Longevity Is One of Our Greatest Gifts

Longevity is a relatively new concept, but should be the cornerstone of any new prosperity planning. Our forebears put most of their life-energy into surviving and did it in a world without credit cards, cable TV, MRIs, mutual funds, or sport-utility vehicles. There were few opportunities for growing one's nest egg outside of company pensions (some 60 percent of American workers are still without private pensions). For them, retirement was a rarity. They were lucky to make it to fifty, much less sixty.

Just because we live longer we have the opportunity to do so much more than the generations of people who came before us. If you live long enough, you can do hundreds of things, but before you consider your mortality, you may need to balance the different parts of your life in addition to working on your financial well-being. What you need to know, however, you probably can identify in a few minutes a week. Here's an exercise to get you off on the right foot:

Personal Ecology Balancing Exercise
Here's a fun and engaging self-survey, meaning there are no right or wrong answers. No salesman will call. Simply reflect on your answers and turn to the next chapter.

1. What is work to you? Is it something that you can leave for an extended period of time and not miss it? When would you leave if you had the chance?

2. If you won the lottery tomorrow, what would you do with the money? How would you spend it? Would you still want or *need* to work at something?

3. If there are areas of your life that are out of balance, what are they? In other words, what are you doing too much of and not enough of? Do you need more quality family time and less time at work? More time for volunteer activities and hobbies?

4. Is there a big project(s) in your life? It can be a specific goal, person you want to help or have a relationship with, or major activity that you would pursue with passion. Write the projects down in order of importance. How would you find the time (and money) to do them?

5. What do you do for spiritual fulfillment? If you're not doing enough of it, how would you do more of it?

6. What's easier to do, make more money or work the same amount (or less) and cut expenses? (The next step will examine this.) Money can bring you wealth, but prosperity takes time (yours).

The answers to these questions will ultimately tell you if you are on the path to a new prosperity. The seeds of change may already be in your hands. Use these observations as you walk through the other self-surveys in this book and begin to shape your new prosperity plan.

Where Do You Stand? What Do You Know and What Do You Do About It?

1. Things are not getting any better in the old workplace. So prepare for some major changes by either educating yourself to do something of value to the world economy or plan an early exit from the workforce.

█

2. If your life is out of balance between work, leisure, and family/community activities, you can rebalance it by adopting a sound personal ecology. Focus on relationships.

█

3. Be honest. What do you need to do to effect this rebalancing? Spend less? Earn more? Work less, save more? There are lots of combinations that will suit the many phases of the life ahead of you.
Enjoy the journey.

Your Financial Portrait: Balancing Your Spending with What You Need for Early Retirement

Money may be the husk of many things, but not the kernel. It brings you food, but not appetite; medicine, but not the health; acquaintances, but not friends; servants, but not faithfulness; days of joy, but not peace or happiness.

—Henrik Ibsen

As a former personnel director for a medium-sized steam-turbine company in New York State, Dick Parker is all too familiar with the bromides that the financial services industry pushes as the most visible "truth" of retirement. It's a fairly simple mantra, used by every brokerage house, insurer, mutual fund, and financial advisor: When you retire, you'll need from 65 percent to 80 percent of your pre-retirement income to live comfortably and not touch the principal of your nest egg. This so-called classic formula is not off the mark for most people, but for Dick—and others like him who have a low-cost lifestyle—early retirement is extremely accessible with relatively little money.

Although Dick is a reserved and intelligent man, the dyed-in-the-wool "65% to 80% rule" strikes him as an interesting bit of fiction. "I think people are able to live on significantly less income in retirement than conventional wisdom suggests. My experience, and that of people I talk to, says many people get by comfortably on $20,000 to $25,000 annually providing their house is paid off and they do not have any debt."

Dick made about $60,000 a year when he retired eight years ago. Since he planned well, he has projected how much money he would need to live comfortably during retirement. One of Dick's major concerns is that he is "having trouble building an elegant fence for my Japanese garden." He's also been somewhat frustrated in getting local school officials to allocate his time as a mentor. They haven't gotten back to him as often as he'd like. He's willing to share his talents and experience and is also a trustee of the local library. In the years he's been retired (since January 1991), he hasn't missed the multiple takeovers and organizational changes of his company, which has been owned by four different conglomerates. He weighed his early-retirement decision for two years prior to leaving, discussing his move with retirees in the community, noting that at the time, "My job didn't have the pizzazz it once did."

As an early retiree (he left when he was sixty), Dick doesn't live an ascetic life. He enjoys visiting his four married children in Rochester (a few hours' drive) and seven grandchildren, and playing tennis, golf, and racquetball. He even splurged on a new car when he left his employer five years early. He's secure enough that he can afford to be generous, by gifting $10,000 to each of his children for college. For some reason, though, you won't find Dick's picture on the cover of any glossy personal-finance magazine. That's because he has no secret strategy. He didn't reap a windfall when his company issued stock, didn't buy and sell real estate for no money down, and he certainly hasn't dabbled in Internet stocks. He credits his comfortable retirement to having no major debts, paying his bills from month to month, and living a modest lifestyle in a small community.

"A lot of people look for a pat formula, but don't apply the rule of reason," he says assuredly. "They don't design a plan that fits them."

If there was such a thing as a boilerplate early-retirement plan, Bill Gates would have it on every computer and it would be on the evening news every night. Unfortunately, the basic rules for a workable new prosperity plan are highly individual, not glamorous, and as such unlikely to arouse much interest from the media or financial advertisers. To dissect the anatomy of such a plan, let's look at Dick's easy approach:

- **Reducing or eliminating debt.** This is the cornerstone of any new prosperity plan. Dick's mortgage is paid off and he doesn't have any significant short-term debt like credit card bills. If you're out of debt, your major living expenses are cut by one-third or more. If this is you, cutting your income at retirement won't crimp your lifestyle. Although you certainly can retire *with* a mortgage, not having one puts a lot of money in your pocket, or, better yet, in your investment vehicles.

- **Fully investing in company retirement plans.** Dick directly invested up to 10 percent of his annual income in his company's 401(k) for eighteen years, mostly in no-brainer stock-index mutual funds, which cheaply and efficiently invest in a broad index of at least five hundred large-company stocks (see step 6 for more details). As a result, he doesn't have to touch the principal portion of his 401(k) funds, which are now invested in money market funds.

- **Beating inflation is critical.** Even though his portfolio is fairly conservatively invested, half in stocks and half in income vehicles, Dick estimates his annual rate of return on his portfolio is 14.7% a year. He surmises it could be higher if he increased the percentage of stocks, but he's comfortable with his investment mix. If inflation is 2% annually (as it is at the time of this writing), he's outpacing it by a factor of seven. That will help build his retirement funds for when he needs them thirty years from now.

- **Health-care costs are covered.** To make sure he had health insurance coverage, Dick continued his company's health plan but pays the lower group rates (vs. an individual plan with premiums up to four times higher). For many early retirees, this is the best and most affordable way of covering health care until you qualify for Medicare when you apply for Social Security (starting at age sixty-five). He also pays for a Medicare supplement policy—Medigap—to cover drug expenses that are not covered by Medicare (as this goes to press). Unless Congress approves Medicare-based coverage for prescription costs, you'll need a plan that covers this often lofty expense as well.

- **Individual stocks provide even more growth.** Dick has also taken the time to learn about investing on his own. He's researched stocks and owns a few hundred shares of companies like Microsoft and Cisco Systems, which have posted the largest gains in his portfolio. Microsoft alone has soared 44% in a year. Dick regards himself as conservative when it comes to the stock market but won't move his money out of it unless something catastrophic happens. "I'm cautious, but reasonably aggressive with the little piece [of cash] I invest," he adds. "I put much more money into stock index mutual funds and buy individual stocks for fun." Since stocks are virtually the only way of beating inflation and obtaining growth of principal, they are the core of growing his new prosperity portfolio. His only safety rule concerning the market is: "I look at what makes me sick to my stomach—maybe a fifteen to twenty percent dip—otherwise I stay in."

- **Cash investments are maintained for safety of principal.** Dick keeps roughly half of his money in a money-market mutual fund and EE U.S. Savings Bonds, which pay the highest possible rates of return. (The other half is in stocks.) He also bought $50,000 of ultra-secure U.S. Treasury notes when they were at 7.25%, which he held to maturity. Although this is not the optimal growth allocation for most retirees, Dick says this mix allows him to sleep at night. He knows he'll have some income he can depend upon even if something happens to the stock market. Other than these income vehicles, he stays out of the volatile (nongovernment) bond market. "I'm not into bonds, I never did understand them. If I'd been in a bond mutual fund a few years back, I would've lost my shirt."

Your Financial Portrait . . . But First
Let's Take a Snapshot

Before you can ask the daunting question "Can I retire?" it's essential that you take a "snapshot" of how much money you have coming in and how you spend it. This is akin to what professional photographers do during a shoot. They'll snap a few Polaroids before using their really expensive film and equipment to see if the lighting, setting, and other particulars are right. This early preparation is necessary for the first phase of your new prosperity plan, which is based on saving enough to finance your new prosperity portfolio. After you've done your snapshot, you can do a more complete financial "portrait." (If you've already done a complete analysis of how much you earn and spend on your own, then you may want to skim this chapter and head to the next one).

Like Dick Parker, you may already be in a position to retire with the money you have now combined with a low-expense lifestyle. You have a great start if you own your own home and cars and don't live high on the hog. In any case, doing a financial snapshot won't hurt. Keep in mind, though, that your financial snapshot tends to be revealing. You'll find out a lot about yourself and your family. Too many of us spend because we believe that by purchasing that home, car, wardrobe, or sound system that we'll be better, smarter, sexier, and more interesting people. We work to spend our money by surrounding ourselves with or immersing ourselves in what our consumer culture claims are life-enhancing objects or activities, which range from beer to health spas.

There's little argument that some things enhance our lives to a great degree: the arts, hobbies and crafts, even bicycles. But the question is to what degree? It's useless to pick at every item we spend money on and make a judgment on it. We have to look at our lifestyle holistically and ask ourselves, "Do all these things I spend money on enhance my/our prosperity?" This way you'll have a clearer insight into your personal ecology. How much do the things you spend money on add to your lives? Spending can easily slip out of balance with your income; when it does, it puts undue pressure on you and your spouse to make more money or make other sacrifices to keep up a lifestyle that reaches beyond your means. Sickness, job loss, and other unforeseen events can put a great deal of stress on our new prosperity plans, but if your savings and spending are balanced, you won't be financially devastated by most of the challenges that crop up. If you make conscious choices on spending and saving, life surprises won't greatly impair your prosperity.

Spending portraits will give you an image of the life-energies— the resources you put into earning money—that might be chasing something that ultimately detracts from your life. A spending portrait, in short, is one of the first steps in attaining your personal ecology: your solid, grounded relationship with the outside world and its many choices that's based on your real needs and goals.

Your Spending Portrait: How Much Does Your Life Cost?

For Dick Parker, doing a spending portrait was simple. He put his expenses down on a piece of paper and figured what he spent on basic living expenses, travel, and other luxury items. This is really all it takes to do a spending portrait, but the real numbers elude us because all too often we can't be honest about how much we spend. Let's assume your credit card is like a magnet. Every time you see an article of clothing, CD, appliance, meal, or vacation you absolutely have to have, it has this irresistible force that pulls it uncontrollably to a cash register. *Swipe.* You got it. Feel better? Of course, not everyone has this attraction to the forces of commerce. But if some of this sounds vaguely familiar, let's examine the forces at work.

Let's begin with the most obvious trappings of our financial selves by asking "How much does my life cost?" What we're interested in now is assigning a "P factor" rating to every major cost item in your monthly pile of bills. The *P*—as in *prosperity*—can be as simple as a plus or minus. If you are so inclined, use a scale from one to ten or letters from A through F. The higher the P factor, the more value this particular item gives to your life. Say you buy a suit. You have a choice between the $500 designer suit and another brand for $250. Does the designer suit give you twice as much value or prosperity? Both items serve the same purpose; how is one more valuable to you?

For example, most homes have a high P factor. Unless you live in a troubled neighborhood or your home needs a lot of work, this typically high P factor is connected to a "high-value" debt. This debt allows you to live where you want in comfort, so it has a durable value. Pull out your latest three credit card bills or checking account statements. Work your way down the list, assigning P factor ratings to every item. Put the list away for a week, then look at it again. Can you make some decisions on how to improve your overall P factor? By doing so, you're not only improving your life, you're spending less and conserving more of your income for your new prosperity plan.

By walking through this exercise you'll be able to tell three things: (1) How much does it cost to sustain my/our present lifestyle item by item? (2) Where can changes be made if the present lifestyle is unsustainable? (3) Which items can be trimmed or eliminated based on their relative P factors and monthly finance charges? (If you do this exercise on a computer, print out a statement.)

Rating Your Biggest Expenses

The second part of your portrait has a little less flexibility, but you can still apply the P factor in determining the value of your largest expenses. You need to rate your "nondiscretionary" expenses, because if you can make a change—and reduce your expenses— you may achieve your new prosperity sooner. After all, if you are to balance your spending with your income, why not look at the whole picture and question where you live and how much it costs to live there? Property taxes, for example, are a fairly large nondiscretionary bill for most of us homeowners. Why not assign a P factor to the value of your local taxes? Pull out your property tax bill. Are you happy with the schools, the water supply, the library, and the roads? If not, would another area provide more value? This begs the question of whether your new prosperity plan involves relocation to where you might combine desired amenities with lower living expenses.

Moving down the list of all your taxes, there's not a lot you can do about most income-related taxes, but keep in mind that payroll taxes (look at your paycheck stub) are adjustable at any time by changing your withholding allowances—the higher the number of allowances, the less money withheld from your paycheck. The IRS form provided to give you guidance is about as useful as a buggy whip in a sports car. So ask your accountant/tax preparer for help, or just look at last year's tax refund. If you have a refund of $1,000 or more, contrary to popular wisdom, that's not really a windfall. What it means is that you've just given the U.S. Treasury an interest-free loan for more than a year. When was the last time Uncle Sam did that for you? Fix the disparity by raising your allowances and withholding less money on your W-2 form.

On the other items, read on for dozens of ways to save money and set aside more funds for your new prosperity plan.

YOUR SPENDING PORTRAIT

Item	Monthly Payment	Total Finance Charges	P Factor
Home Mortgage/Rent	_____	_____	_____
Home Remodeling	_____	_____	_____
Home-Equity Loan	_____	_____	_____
Personal Loans	_____	_____	_____
Installment Loans	_____	_____	_____
Non-A/V Appliances (if financed)	_____	_____	_____

Item	Monthly Payment	Total Finance Charges	P Factor
Sound System/Television	_____	_____	_____
Computers	_____	_____	_____
Internet Service (fees)	_____	_____	_____
Software	_____	_____	_____
Movies, Cable TV	_____	_____	_____
Satellite Dish (include hardware)	_____	_____	_____
Vehicle 1	_____	_____	_____
Vehicle 2	_____	_____	_____
Vehicle 3	_____	_____	_____
Boats	_____	_____	_____
RVs	_____	_____	_____
Motorcycles	_____	_____	_____
Bicycles	_____	_____	_____
Food	_____	_____	_____
Clothing	_____	_____	_____
Dry Cleaning	_____	_____	_____
Vacations	_____	_____	_____
Gifts (birthdays, holidays, etc.)	_____	_____	_____
Hobbies/Crafts	_____	_____	_____
Eating Out	_____	_____	_____
Health Club/Spas	_____	_____	_____

Item	Monthly Payment	Total Finance Charges	P Factor
Misc. Entertainment (plays, events)	――	――	――
Non-Discretionary Expenses			
Property Taxes	――	――	――
Income Taxes (federal/state/local)	――	――	――
Payroll Taxes (FICA/insurance)	――	――	――
Health Insurance	――	――	――
Homeowners/Renters Insurance	――	――	――
Vehicle Insurance (all premiums)	――	――	――
Life Insurance (annual premium)	――	――	――
Home Repairs/Maintenance	――	――	――
Utilities (gas, electric, phone, water)	――	――	――
Assessments (if applicable)	――	――	――
Commuting (train/car/bus)	――	――	――
Personal Maintenance (hair)	――	――	――

Item	Monthly Payment	Total Finance Charges	P Factor
Nonreimbursed Health Care (out-of-pocket medical, dental, eye care)	————	————	————
Child Care	————	————	————
Elder Care (parents, grandparents)	————	————	————
School Expenses (tuition, books, etc.)	————	————	————
Emergency Expenses	————	————	————

TOTAL MONTHLY EXPENSES ————————

This is what you're spending now. Can you make any adjustments? If you were retired, which items would not be on the list? Keep these numbers handy, we'll come back to them later.

Do You Have a Spending Problem?

When it comes to the way we can spend money, in the valley of temptation we are all mountaineers. If the spending portrait you completed is not revealing enough for you, here's a questionnaire you can use to see where you stand. This benchmark self-survey will tell you if you have spending woes.

1. Are you spending most of your income to pay bills and therefore don't save anything for yourself and family? The first ground rule of a new prosperity plan is to *pay yourself first.* That means pulling money from your regular income and putting it in a retirement vehicle of some kind.

2. Do you borrow money to pay nonmortgage or transportation debt? You'll need to eliminate this situation if you are to retire early.

3. Do you think that making the "minimum payment" on your monthly credit card bills will ever pay off the balance of what you owe? It won't. It goes to pay off finance charges. Pay off the principal.

4. Have you been forced to borrow to pay bills? If so, you need to consolidate and restructure your debt.

5. Do you keep track of all your expenses? If not, do you have any idea how much they are relative to all your sources of income? If you're working to pay off creditors, prosperity will elude you.

If you answered "yes" to more than three questions, then read on. There are hundreds of things you can do to cut your expenses. But first it's important to know how much you make. Your income portrait is the other half of the balancing of the books for your new prosperity. Ideally, you have more money coming in than going out every month. If you don't now, you may need to make some "prosperity adjustments" to get you on the launching pad for new prosperity and early retirement.

Balancing Your Lifestyle: Your Income Portrait

Let's say, for example, that your spending is way out of balance with your income; that is, it exceeds it by thousands of dollars and you are financing your lifestyle with credit cards and short-term debt like installment loans. Don't panic or write off early retirement. You can rebalance your financial picture by making some decisions based on the P factors you assigned to some of your cost items. It involves a basic formula: If your total expenses exceed your income (pencil the figures in in the table below), then you'll need to ask yourself some questions about how to make adjustments. The P-factor you assigned to the items you spend money on will help. Consider cutting as many low P-factor items as you can and see if, at the end of this exercise, your income is greater than your expenses. It's that simple.

A key part of your income portrait involves a balancing act as well. If you're not happy with the way you *earn* your money, then you may lean heavy on the spending side, seeking satisfaction in purchases. Let's say you've done well as a lawyer, stockbroker, salesperson, or anyone who has somehow benefited from the U.S. business boom over the last twenty years. But you didn't feel right about how you earned that money. It robbed a bit of your soul. Or the hours kept you away from your family. So you made up for your dissatisfaction and guilt by spending lavishly on sports cars, Caribbean vacations, $1,000 suits, and eating out three nights week. To square this income with your personal ecology now, you'll find it useful to assign a P factor to how you earn certain kinds of income. While making money is good, assigning a lower P factor to any income will remind you how it weighs against other sources in your overall income scheme. You may find that profiting from stocks, bonds, or rental property has a much higher P factor to you than your livelihood. If that's the case, work through the advanced planning on creating an income stream in the next chapter. For now, though, let's look at your income:

YOUR BASIC INCOME PORTRAIT

Item	Monthly Amount	P Factor
Salary/Wages	————	————
Commissions	————	————
Bonuses/Tips	————	————
Self-Employment or Part-Time Work	————	————

Item	Monthly Amount	P Factor
Rental Income	————	————
Child Support/Alimony	————	————
Hobbies/Crafts	————	————
Bonds	————	————
Inheritance	————	————
Disability Payments	————	————
Investment Income	————	————
Realized Capital Gains (from business/stocks/real estate, etc., minus capital gains taxes where applicable)	————	————

TOTAL MONTHLY INCOME – ————————

TOTAL MONTHLY EXPENSES = ————————

PROSPERITY ADJUSTMENT   ————————

The total is your prosperity adjustment, *or what's left at the end of the month after all the bills are paid and investments made. If you have a surplus, invest it. If you come up short (that is, you have a negative number), you need to make adjustments to your spending portrait and read the next section.* NOTE: Step 2 and the next chapter will allow you to improve your prosperity adjustment by cutting expenses, so read through step 3 and come back to this total and revise expenses where appropriate.

Punching the Big Tickets First

The only thing worse than paying bills is *not* paying them. For too many households, money is a frequent visitor who never stays long enough to feel welcome. If you made it out of the previous section with a positive prosperity adjustment—you're paying all your bills on time and have enough money left over to invest—then you can probably still save some more money for your new prosperity plan and early retirement. If you have no further conflicts with your spending plan, you may skip to step 3, where I explore financial planning issues in greater depth. In any case, go back over both your expenses and income a few times to see if you missed anything. Cross reference with your pay stubs, mutual fund/banking statements, and credit card bills.

If you have too many expenses to be covered by your income and are looking for a way of balancing your lifestyle, you'll be happy to hear that nearly every big-ticket item can be scaled back in some way. You can definitely save on your mortgage and home expenses, transportation costs, and other items by running through the following checklists. Let's start with your home expenses, perhaps your biggest-ticket item.

Save Big on Your Mortgage

With interest rates dropping over the past decade and a half, it hasn't been unusual to see mortgage rates at thirty-year lows. As a result, millions of homeowners refinanced, upgraded, or downscaled this hefty expense. You may be able to take advantage of some savings here. Take a look at your most recent mortgage statement. Is the rate at least a point above what you could get on the market now? It's not true that you need a two-point spread between your present note and prevailing rates in order for refinancing to make sense. Any form of refinancing that ultimately puts more money in your pocket—money you can use to fund your prosperity plan—makes a lot of sense. If you know you're going to stay in your home, refinance—but make sure you're getting the best rate and the lowest-possible fees. A low rate should be accompanied by no points and little in the way of "junk fees," such as origination, document handling, service, and other charges that are simply pure profit for banks. The Internet is a good source for tracking down low mortgage rates, but watch out for middlemen who take a slice of the loan. You may be better off working with a local mortgage broker, who doesn't directly issue the loans but finds the lowest-cost loan from a variety of lenders. There's usually a generous listing of lenders and loan rates in the real estate section of your local newspapers—typically in weekend editions.

Which mortgage term you choose can also save you money. Again, the one that will make most sense for you depends on how long you're going to stay in your home. If you're headed for the Sun Belt soon as a permanent resident, choose an *adjustable-rate* mortgage (ARM). These loans provide the lowest rates for short periods of time, but can be converted into *fixed-rate* loans with terms from fifteen to thirty years. The lowest fixed-rate loan is typically a 15-year note, and you'll pay less in total interest in the 30-year version. Again, the term is tied in to how long you plan to stay in your home. For example, say you know you're going to retire within the next five to twenty years and refinance with a 15-year note. On a $100,000 fixed-rate loan at 8 percent per year, you'll pay $90,000 less than you would on a 30-year note. That's a big chunk of potential retirement funds!

While you're tweaking your mortgage costs, other savings are possible by:

- Saving your escrow funds in an interest-bearing account and paying your taxes yourself. You'll not only earn interest on this often considerable amount of money, you'll avoid common "escrow errors," where banks overestimate the amount needed for taxes and insurance.

- Asking for a discount on the mortgage rate if the banks you approach accept payments electronically or by direct deposit. You can save up to half of a percentage point on the annual finance rate.

- Choosing to pay your mortgage off early by doubling the principal payment on your monthly check to the bank. By making this one extra payment each month you can often trim half the total payments off your mortgage loan and save thousands in interest payments. *With double principal payments on a 30-year note you can pay off your loan in fifteen years!*

Your Relocation Scenario

You may have been fantasizing for a long time about living near a beach, a golf course, or in a climate where snow shoveling is not required. If so, scout out and choose a location that you can afford for your early retirement. Examine state income tax rates. Some states, such as Florida and Nevada, have no state income taxes, but you should take a look at housing and transportation costs in the areas you choose to relocate. They can make up or eclipse the difference you save on income tax if you are not careful. It's also important to choose a location with good transportation (airports, trains, bus routes), health care (hospitals and clinics), and cultural amenities (universities, symphonies, arts festivals). If you pick a beautiful spot in the mountains, but it takes your loved ones two days to get there, then the value of that relocation may be somewhat diminished. Nevertheless, if you have a place in mind, see what it costs to live there.

Let's say you have your spending under control. You can make your new prosperity possible sooner by picking a low-cost part of the country (as opposed to a high-cost area, noted in the table that follows). How much can you save just by relocating to an area with a lower cost of living? According to a Georgia State University study (the RETIRE project), you can save up to six figures a year in living expenses. For example, if you moved from the expensive Palo Alto, California, area (or anywhere in the Bay Area or Silicon Valley, for that matter) to Santa Fe, New Mexico, and you are presently living on an income of $250,000 a year, you can save up to $125,000 by doing this relocation downsizing. If you are in the middle of the income spectrum, moving from Chicago on $75,000 a year to Fort Myers, Florida, will save you $31,272 a year. Of course, you don't have to do anything cold turkey. Try out some of your alternative locations on vacation or rent there for six months to get a feel for the area and what you'll spend living there. You may be able to live there part-time and still save some money. My parents, for example, live in Chicago from May through December, then head down to their "honeymoon condo" in Florida, where they act like teenagers and socialize with a host of friends and neighbors who have also relocated part-time.

For guidelines, here's the relative living costs and some popular-but-affordable places for relocation.

SAMPLE LIVING COSTS BY AREA

Metro Area	Rent (monthly)	Home Energy Cost
New York City	$2,920	$187
Boston	$1,078	$139
Los Angeles	$778	$120
Denver	$740	$82
Atlanta	$700	$94
Portland, Oregon	$673	$79
Houston	$667	$109
Minneapolis	$620	$101

Source: American Chamber of Commerce Researchers Association, 1998

Keep in mind these are just sample costs, not averages. You can obviously pay a lot more or less depending on the community, type of housing, and your lifestyle. You can, however, conclude that housing costs are probably highest in the Northeast and along the California coast, and lowest in the Midwest, South, and Southeast. These numbers also don't take into account local health-care costs (you can make the same assumptions made for housing costs), transportation, or other amenities. These lower-cost areas, however, have thriving cultural communities, plenty of universities, and ample health-care facilities. Energy costs are also highly variable depending on the type of housing and how efficient your heating and cooling systems are. These are all key factors to consider when planning your relocation.

AFFORDABLE AND INTERESTING
RETIREMENT SITES

Location	Advantages
Green Valley, Arizona	Desert and mountains combine for a moderate climate.
Oxford, Mississippi	Inexpensive and home to the University of Mississippi.
University Triangle, North Carolina	Located near Raleigh-Durham, plenty of universities, golf courses, and cultural activities.
Palm Coast, Florida	Located between Daytona Beach and St. Augustine, lots of beach, less-expensive housing, and not too many people.
Hot Springs/Mena, Arkansas	Mountains, universities, and lakes cradle areas of inexpensive homes and many amenities.
Georgetown, Texas	A quiet place in the hill country near Austin's high-tech corridor and the University of Texas.
Durango, Colorado	Mountains and a four-season climate with lots of Old West charm and geological wonders.
Las Vegas, Nevada	Inexpensive housing and plenty of entertainment, mountains, and desert.
Paradise, California	Sitting in a forest near the Sierra Nevada, lots of recreation.
Ashland, Oregon	Home to a famous Shakespeare festival and near mountains, lakes, rivers, and universities.

Location	Advantages
Boise, Idaho	A midsize city with a relatively mild climate near mountains and amenities.
Bloomington, Indiana	Home to Indiana University, affordable and friendly.

Source: "The Best Places to Retire in America," by John Howells, author of *Where to Retire* (Globe-Pequot, 1998), as condensed from *Consumers Digest,* September/ October 1998.

Transfixed by Transportation? You Can Save More Than You Think

It wasn't too long ago when you could buy a reasonably reliable car for a few hundred dollars. Today it's commonplace for a family financing or leasing two vehicles to be spending $700 a month— often more than their mortgage—for these depreciating assets. According to the American Automobile Association, the average yearly expense for a midsized auto is $4,500 a year, which represents the second-highest expense in many American households. Can we get that number down to raise some new prosperity dollars? Yes!

My dad, who was able to retire at fifty-nine, was constantly on the lookout for cheap and decent cars that would run with relatively little maintenance. He was so frugal with his transportation budget for such a long time that I used to kid him that to save money on gas he'd even drive without headlights and turn off the dashboard lights at night. I don't think he ever went that far, but he did go through a wide variety of cars from a Chevy Vega (a profound waste of sheet metal) to a Volvo. His was an ongoing experiment of finding the cheapest, most reliable car. The ones I got were certified clunkers, many of which I inherited in college (for modest fees) and during my first newspaper reporting jobs. I was happy to get them most of the time. One of my favorite cars was a 1966 Pontiac Tempest with an unabashed V-8 under the hood. It *flew*. Once it was even stolen from the parking lot of E.J. Korvette's department store, where I worked during college in the late 1970s. Apparently someone just stole it for a joyride because the police found it a few days later in a nearby suburb with all of the parts still intact.

Spending money imprudently on transportation can derail your early-retirement plan, and you won't even realize it. Today the average price of a new car is around $20,000, which is roughly what my parents paid for their *house* in 1956. But when you add in financing, insurance, fuel, maintenance, and licensing fees, the modern new vehicle can be an even greater drain on your ability to fund a new prosperity plan.

An even bigger financial demon is the concept of *depreciation*, where your four-wheel assets are constantly dropping in value all the time you are paying interest to finance its purchase and pouring money into fixing it and fueling it. It's a losing proposition no matter how you look at it. More important, in terms of being able to fund an early retirement, overspending on transportation will impede your new prosperity because of the *time value* of money. In other words, the money you could be using to grow your retirement kitty is going into an asset that is losing money every single day and is worth 40 percent less in two years' time.

The quickest way for most two-car families and couples to halve their transportation budget is to live with one vehicle or buy used cars. In retirement, you may need only one means of transportation, if you and your significant other are home most of the time. If this is possible, go ahead and figure in the savings of not paying for financing/leasing, insurance, fuel, maintenance, and cleaning. If you need two vehicles, you can still save some money. Transportation costs go beyond just buying or leasing a vehicle. Again, you have to figure in *depreciation,* or the value of your initial investment dropping over time. It's like inflation in reverse. Figure that a dollar invested in a vehicle (except for a handful of cars) will be worth sixty cents two years from now. That's money you can't recover, reinvest, or ever see again. Depreciation is only one part of the transportation equation. Add to that fuel, maintenance, insurance (you pay more based on the sticker price, theft rate, where you live, and how old you are), and the total cost of financing. That $20,000 vehicle can be a $32,000 proposition over five years when all the costs are figured in—none are which are recoverable. Here's a quick example of saving money by buying a used car.

NEW VS. USED VEHICLES: YOUR NET SAVINGS

A $20,000 New Car Compared with an $11,616 Used Car

Cost	New	Used
Yearly Payments (with interest)	$3,501	$3,241
Monthly Payments	$564	$310
First-Year Depreciation	$5,000	$1,626
Total Depreciation During Ownership	$10,010	$5,409
Total Interest on Financing	$2,306	$1,554

Source: www.smartcalc.com (CalcBuilder on www.kiplinger.com)

The used car is the same model as the new car, only three years older and with $8,384 of depreciation subtracted (money you didn't have to lose).

The Savings over Time

Okay, so the $261 yearly difference between the two cars' total payments seems like a trivial amount. Let's see, however, what the time value of that difference is and what it could mean added to your new prosperity fund:

$261 over 5 years (let's say this is how long you own the car) = $1,305
Invested for 20 years @ 8% annual rate of return =
$3,543 in a taxable account
$6,087 in a tax-deferred account

Okay, so $6,087 won't make the difference between a golf-course condo and a stuffy apartment, so let's amplify the example a bit.

New Prosperity Savings: Eliminating an expensive vehicle (or second/third vehicle)

Let's say you own an "intermediate four-door sport-utility vehicle (SUV)," which would be a Ford Explorer, Jeep Cherokee, or a Toyota 4-Runner. According to Intellichoice.com, the five-year ownership cost for this class of vehicles is $31,055. That's what you're paying to finance it, fuel it, insure and maintain it. Keep in mind the sticker price (without loading it up with options) is around $25,000, which is not the most you can spend on an SUV (you can spend up to $90,000), but it's somewhere toward the low end. What would happen if you sold that vehicle, or simply didn't buy one in the first place, and invested that $31,055?

> In twenty years that money, earning a modest 8 percent annual rate of return, would be worth:
> *$84,302 in a taxable account*
> *$144,746 in a tax-deferred account (28% marginal income-tax bracket, 8% state)*

Are we talking real money yet? We're not even figuring the difference between the more expensive vehicles ($30,000 and up) and cheaper wheels and what you could save over time just by investing the savings. Of course, the numbers really get huge when you invest the savings over forty years (if you're retiring at fifty and you live to at least ninety). Nevertheless, you get the idea that one (or more) spending decisions on *vehicles alone* can impact the rest of your life. If you can make this decision now—and save the difference—your lifestyle will be improved because you'll have more money in the future.

I have nothing against cars, trucks, or vans. Just buy the one that suits your needs and gets you where you're going. Spending less on a vehicle will ensure prosperity in real dollars in a short period of time. Just because I really want to be sure you understand what's at stake when you visit the next car dealer, here's two examples of how not buying the top-of-line vehicle in a class can save you big dollars over just five years:

PROSPERITY AND TRANSPORTATION: TWO COMPARISONS

1999 Jeep Cherokee SE (2wd, 4dr, 2.5 L, 5-speed)

List Price: $ 16,480

Financing: $4,065

Depreciation (1998–2002): $7,758

Total Cost*: $28,531

1999 Land Rover/Range Rover 4.6 HSE (4wd, 4.6 L, 4-speed)

List Price: $63,500

Financing: $13,163

Depreciation: $30,394

Total Cost: $72,393

Model: 1999 Honda Accord DX Sedan (3L, 5-speed manual)

List Price: $15,100

Financing: $3,239

Depreciation: $4,474

Total Cost: $22,512

Model: Nissan Maxima GLF Sedan (3L, 4-speed auto)

List Price: $26,899

Financing: $5,504

Depreciation: $13,233

Total Cost: $35,297

Source: IntelliChoice, Inc.'s *Car and Truck Costs Guides 1999*. For more detailed information on the best values in cars, check out www.consumersdigest.com, www.intellichoice.com, or www.autobytel.com.

Total cost includes five-year depreciation, financing, insurance, state fees, fuel, maintenance, and repairs.

Although the four models chosen in these examples aren't exactly apples-to-apples comparisons, they are similar types of vehicles. I'm not making any suggestion as to which offer the best quality. I simply want to show you the outrageous variations in how much money you can spend between something that's fairly basic and something that's at or near the top of the line. Is there a good reason for spending the money you burn in depreciating a Land Rover over five years, when you could buy *two* new Honda Accords? Even if you're looking for a nonluxury sedan, why is there three times as much depreciation in owning the arguably nicer Nissan Maxima versus the spartan-but-reliable Accord? The $12,785 difference between the two cars would be a hefty jump start on a new prosperity plan. So, would you rather have those fancy wheels or be living that life you've only dared dream of five years earlier than you even thought possible?

My moral: Buy for your needs, not for your ego. Vehicles are basic transportation. For my most recent set of wheels, I bought a 1996 Geo Metro LSI for $11,000, which is one of the least expensive cars on the road. I even saved $1,000 on my purchase buying it through an auto broker. Before I bought the Geo, I sold a 1986 Acura Integra (one of the best cars I ever bought) with 188,000 miles on it after eight years of happy ownership. To acquire it, I traded a VW Golf and paid $5,000 to the (then) auto editor of *Consumers Digest,* my colleague and friend Jim Gorzelany, who has since been promoted to managing editor at the magazine. When I was ready for a new car—and wanted a four-door automatic with the latest safety features—I could have bought a new Acura for $22,000 or bought a less-snazzy Honda Civic for $18,000. Here are some other smart vehicle tips for saving money and adding to your early-retirement cache:

- **Lease versus buy, which is the better deal?** Lease only if you can write off the expense for your business and you drive less than 12,000 to 15,000 miles a year. By far, the best strategy is to "buy and hold." Get a reliable vehicle at a reasonable price (usually a year or two on old cars so that someone else has eaten the depreciation), maintain it well, and hold on to it for at least six years. Detroit would rather have you buy or lease a new car every year, but is it worth working more years to get it? Think about it.

■ **Cash or finance?** If you have the cash, can get a good price on reliable wheels, and have your prosperity plan fully funded, go the cash route. You can get a bigger discount from the dealer and save on total financing costs. It's also cheaper than leasing. If you have to finance, go for the shortest term with the most amount of money down. Again, you'll save on total finance expenses. If you can't swing the monthly payment, don't finance your vehicle with a home-equity loan (even though it's tax deductible at a lower interest rate). If you default, you'll lose the car—and the house.

■ **Choose a car with a relatively low price, low depreciation rate, maintenance, insurance, and fuel costs.** I'm a little biased, but the best vehicle "value" comparisons among similar models are found in the January/February issue of *Consumers Digest* (updated every year) or at www.consumersdigest.com.

Credit Cards: What You Absolutely Need to Know

With 1.4 *billion* pieces of plastic out there, this $500 billion industry is not going away soon. Everybody—from your alumni association to your airline—wants to sign you up all the time. Am I right? That means, if you're like me, four to six pieces of mail *per day* (out of ten) are solicitations for credit cards, lines of credit, or home-equity loans. The "average" credit card debt per household per month is about $2,000, but the best card debt is zero. That means you use a credit card to borrow within the grace period of 25 days and pay it off every month. I'm sure you've heard that before, but I can't stress how important this little rule is. Better yet, make it pay *you.* Here are some little-advertised truths about using credit cards.

■ **You only need one credit card.** I know the banks and finance companies hate this idea. Get one low or no-fee card and pay the balance off each month.

- Make it a "rebate" card that pays you back in credits for cars, airline miles, or merchandise credits. Choose one card and stick with it. That way you avoid all finance charges and nuisance fees and get something back. Consult Bankcard Holders of America's credit card lists for the best deals (703-389-5445) or check out www.ramresearch.com.

- If you need to consolidate credit card debt, do it on one low-interest card or home-equity loan. Pay it off each month a bit at a time. Cut up the old cards and send letters to the banks saying you want to close your account and line of credit. Throw out and recycle every new mail solicitation. If you feel you might be tempted by what's inside don't even open the envelope.

- Consult a credit counselor or fee-only financial planner if you just can't get out from under your debt. There are thousands of specialists across the country willing to help (see Resources at the end of this book).

- Stop shopping on impulse. Make a list before you go shopping anywhere. On the list make two columns headed: "Must Have" (food, eyeglasses, etc.) and "Don't Need but Want" (everything that's nonessential). Put the list in a drawer and take a walk. Pull it out the next day and see what you can live without—and how your spending will dip.

Those Little Items That Add Up: Other Ways to Save

MISCELLANEOUS SAVINGS CAN FUEL YOUR NEW PROSPERITY PLAN

Monthly Spending

Use these suggestions or fill in your own monthly expenditures.

By paying off my credit cards   I could save $200

By bringing my lunch to work   I could save $200

By forgoing my latte fix   I could save $ 60

TOTAL: $460

Expected average annual return on your savings: 8%

After one year, your total savings will be $5,759.20.

After five years, your total savings will be $33,212.00.

After ten years, your total savings will be $77, 464.00.

Source: www.Quicken.com/saving

Thanks to the miracle of the Internet, you can shop for virtually anything and save thousands of dollars (see Resources at the back of book). You can also use your Yellow Pages to shop locally. Here are some tips to help you realign your spending plan:

- Eat out less; pay cash for every meal.

- Buy clothes once a year out of season to replace worn-out articles only.

- Plan your travel by shopping for the best fares, packages, and lodging on the Internet or through travel agents (my favorite sites are www.expedia.com, www.previewtravel.com, and www.travelocity.com).

- If you need to remodel your home, choose licensed contractors with references and never pay all the cash up front. Never take the lowest bid, either.

- Save on auto insurance premiums by raising all of your deductibles. Raising deductibles on comprehensive and collision from $250 to $1,000 may save more than one-third on your insurance bills. Buy cars that are inexpensive to insure and keep a clean driving record.

- Shop for insurance (term life, homeowners, medical) through the Internet for a wide range of insurers and better premiums or through independent brokers.

- Buy energy-efficient appliances and furnaces when your old ones wear out. If you're remodeling, add insulation to the walls and ceiling and install "low-e" windows. Watch your heating/cooling bills drop hundreds of dollars a year.

Let's Review a Bit: Prosperity Savings Subtotal

Now's a good time to total up any monthly savings you've achieved from the reassessment on spending that you've done in the previous sections.

Mortgage (refinance, etc.)   _____

Relocation   _____

Transportation   _____

Credit-Card Debt   _____

Reduced Misc. Spending   _____

NOW ADD UP YOUR TOTAL PROSPERITY SAVINGS   _____

NOW SUBTRACT THESE SAVINGS FROM YOUR
TOTAL MONTHLY EXPENSES (PAGE 29) –   _____

POSSIBLE PROSPERITY SAVINGS =   _____

Are you closer to your goal in balancing income with spending? Are you running a surplus that you can save or invest?

You Can Change Your Lifestyle: The P Factor Revisited

If the menu at the restaurant says "all you can eat," most of us will eat more. In the same vein, many of us tend to have a buffet attitude when it comes to material goods. We will spend beyond our incomes because it's so easy to overextend our spending appetites with credit. For most people, however, real wealth is accumulated only if they spend a lot less than what they make. That doesn't mean you have to live like a pauper, or measure your wealth by the size of your foyer or car, or even by your bank account. Instead, you measure it by the freedom to do what you want when you want. You may now realize with this new rule that the house on the

NEW PROSPERITY TIP

One of the first steps to new prosperity is to pay off any outstanding loans (that are non-tax-deductible). Being debt-free is an important goal.

golf course, the luxury car with leather seats, the wardrobe with the walk-in closet, and the "adventure vacations" may not equate with prosperity if you have no time for your loved ones or the ability to walk away from work any time you like.

You can either make a big production of showing people how you spend your resources or reinvest them in your own prosperity, which is much less visible but much more life-enriching for you and your family. Sure, satellite TV and a big sound system are great. Lots of channels, lots of sound. A trip to a Caribbean island is even better. Lots of sand, sailboats, and palm trees. A vacation that packs a lot of memories. Daring. But take some time to think of these things as you are sitting in your office and you would rather be somewhere else. Then how much are these things worth? How much did you have to work to pay for them and what did they give you in return? Did they add or subtract from your feeling of wealth and prosperity? We harken back to the P factor, or the sum total of how things you paid for *added* to your total prosperity. If you're looking at a negative number or rating, then you need to make some decisions. If you are already spending money on what gives you the highest P factors and saving enough money to retire as early as you want, the next chapter will help you make some critical decisions on how and when to engage your prosperity plan.

Use this book to help you realign your goals of early retirement. Cutting spending and improving savings is just one way to get there. Creating a balanced personal ecology will help you ignore what your neighbors or the rest of the country are spending and you will attain a new prosperity at an earlier age.

Checkpoints for Your New Prosperity Plan

1. Is your spending portrait a cloudy image? Do you know what you're spending money on and the value you receive from it?

2. What's the prosperity (P) factor for your major cost items? Are they adding or subtracting from your life?

3. If you have a problem with debt—particularly credit cards— have you come up with a plan to scale back the most onerous debts?

4. Do you have a clear portrait of other expenses in your life? Once you do, you can kick your prosperity plan into high gear.

Get the Life You Want Now by Structuring an Income Stream

Whether industrial, financial, or commercial, the corporation is considered the primary instrument of "progress," although just what progress means is never clear.

—Thomas Berry, *The Dream of the Earth*

When his father's retail furniture store closed for the evening, Don Kraft cranked up the phonograph and swayed to a Latin beat with his dance teacher. Against a backdrop of Maytags and Frigidaires in Huntington, West Virginia, a modest though warm-spirited metropolis in the heart of Appalachia, in July of 1953 he was learning the mambo, the dance with which he was going to find a wife. "We simply ran out of nice, Jewish girls in Huntington, so my dad's business partner's wife told me to go to Miami. The travel agent said you couldn't go to Miami without learning how to mambo, so that's why I took the lessons."

After spending a small fortune on mambo lessons ($65), Don was determined not to waste time with any girl who was not similarly skilled. After a tour in the air force, a college degree, and working in his father's furniture/appliance store, along with the mambo lessons, he was ready for matrimony. When he spotted a woman he found out was named Gloria at the Nautilus Hotel in Miami, the question was direct and purposeful: "Do you mambo?" A month later they were engaged and married the following January.

As a newly married man at twenty-nine, he needed a steady income and a job where he could use his degrees in mathematics, so he joined IBM in 1957. Big Blue hired him on as an "applied science representative" in its Columbus, Ohio, office. With the heady growth of IBM and the burgeoning computer business, Don was determined to plan for an early retirement at a time when few workers even dared broach the subject.

Immersing himself in the *Wall Street Journal* and financial reports, he spent two hours a day researching stocks. He bought his employer's stock through the company plan and invested in companies like G.D. Searle (now part of Monsanto) because it produced the first birth-control pill. He bought a three-ring binder and recorded every dividend payment of his stocks, recorded expenses, logged his net worth (assets minus debts) on a regular basis, and absorbed any news on the market. Don's stock buying followed a simple formula: invest in well-managed companies with earnings growth that doubled in five years (this is one of the basics of stock investing practiced by most investment clubs).

As Don's enthusiasm for an early-retirement portfolio increased, so did his knowledge. He performed future value calculations on what his portfolio would be worth down the road at present rates of return. He devoured all the materials at hand in the local library and used that ancient instrument the slide rule to figure rates of return. "The library was better than any brokerage house," he recalls, reflecting on the quality of information he could get free.

Although Don reached a $500,000 net worth in the mid-1970s (about fifteen years after he first started investing), inflation started to rage. He realized he wasn't going to have enough money to cement his lifestyle and provide for the education and weddings of his three daughters, Beverly, Judi, and Lisa. Then in the late 1970s, life threw him a curve. His father-in-law died, leaving a profitable photo-engraving business behind that ran three shifts a day and employed twenty workers. Somebody in the family had to run it. By now Don was working as an instructor for IBM, but figured he could manage some of the business during lunch and after work, since it was only a few blocks away from his base at IBM. At forty-seven, he had plenty of energy to duck in the shop before work, then head over to IBM for a full day's work, then come back to the shop after 5 P.M. He also fully invested in IBM's profit-sharing pension plan with the family business. He ran the business with a brother-in-law (who co-managed and did the books) for ten years as a second job in his off hours; he considered planning his investments his "third job." Although this work schedule was stressful, the investments it allowed him to build eventually gave Don the financial freedom to leave what was then one of the most secure jobs in American industry with the confidence that it was the right move and he could support himself and his family.

After taking some sidetracks with margin accounts and stock options, Don went back to the basics of his retirement plan. "I realized the broker was making more money than I was in options and I was taking all of the risk." By 1980, Don had more than a million dollars put away and resigned from IBM at the age of fifty-three, even though he wasn't fully vested in the IBM retirement plan and was making around $40,000 a year—a decent salary for the time.

Although he planned and invested meticulously for early retirement, Don regrets that he didn't figure in health-care costs, which he had to cover through costly individual policies until he qualified for Medicare. (He never regrets buying the mambo lessons, however.)

Don's plan is far from unusual nor is it particularly complicated. He kept good track of expenses, never spent extravagantly on anything, and focused on growth stocks for his portfolio. To track expenses, he wrote down every expenditure he made in a ledger and employed a novel use of credit cards: He used them to track all of his family's expenses, but paid them off every month. That way, Don had a reliable record of everything they were spending. He bought and used the first IBM personal computer and spreadsheet programs to detail every penny coming in and going out of his portfolio. Here's what he did and what you can do to maximize your new prosperity plan:

- **Buy and hold on to growth stock.** Don invested heavily in one of the premier growth stocks of the last forty years (IBM)—and held on. Even when IBM was buffeted in the late 1980s, he clung to his largest holding. Recently he saw IBM skyrocket 24 points in a single day when the market rediscovered the lumbering giant as a major merchant on the Internet. Don estimates until this year he's sold no more than 20 shares since he first bought IBM in the late 1950s.

- **Keep careful records and plan well.** Don planned carefully by tracking all of his expenses and investments. He even wrote programs for spreadsheets before portfolio-management programs existed.

- **Buy stocks with solid management.** Other major growth stocks with solid management rounded out Don's portfolio: Intel, Coca-Cola, Procter & Gamble, Walgreen's, Glaxo Holdings, General Electric, Compaq are some of his top holdings. Most of them have toed the line and doubled every five years; the tech stocks often double every two years.

- **Focus on compounded return.** Concentrating on compound annual rate of return, Don could project how his money was growing and if it was keeping up with his 15% annual rate of return goal. At that rate, your investment doubles in five years, which is a standard objective for most growth stocks.

- **Share success.** Most of all, Don did his planning to help his family and ensure a fulfilling retirement. He gifts stock to his children and grandchildren. He is extremely active, serves as vice president of the board of a symphony orchestra and has traveled across the globe.

Tracking What You Have:
Phase One of Prosperity Planning

So what kind of life do you want now and what do you need to get there? Typically, financial planners total up all of your assets and subtract your liabilities to come up with a "net worth." Unfortunately, that's not a true model of wealth because you can't access all your assets as if they were cash. Mortgage debt is listed as a liability, but it can also be seen as an investment because you are building equity. And there may be other assets that you can't easily value. For example, some families invest heavily in rental real estate, but until they start selling buildings and subtracting selling costs, they really don't know how much they have. Or, if you have a business partnership or equity interest, it's only worth what somebody is willing to pay for it, so it's hard to say how much is really available for your prosperity plan.

Let's do a little tally of your assets to see where you stand. In the following worksheet, you'll see "Liquid" and "Illiquid" investments. The tax-deferred accounts are often thought of as illiquid because the IRS imposes a 10% penalty plus income tax if you withdraw money from these accounts prior to reaching age 59½. There are, however, ways around that rule if you withdraw your money in "substantial, equal payments according to IRS schedules." More on that later. For now, let's see how much you have.

HOW MUCH DO YOU HAVE NOW?
YOUR STARTING PROSPERITY PORTFOLIO

Resource	Total Value/ Monthly Income	Rate of Return (Annual %)
Liquid Investments		
Stock Mutual Funds	_____	_____
Bond Mutual Funds	_____	_____
Individual Stocks	_____	_____
Bonus	_____	_____

Resource	Total Value/ Monthly Income	Rate of Return (Annual %)
Municipal Bonds/Funds	————	————
Investment Club Shares	————	————
Commodities	————	————
Rental Real Estate Income	————	————
Real Estate Mutual Funds	————	————
Life Insurance Cash Value	————	————
Treasury Bonds/Notes/Bills	————	————
Corporate Bonds (in Mutual Funds)	————	————
Other Bonds	————	————
Cash Accounts		
Savings Accounts	————	————
Money Market Bank Accounts	————	————
Money Market Mutual Funds	————	————
Short-Term Treasury Bills	————	————
Checking	————	————
Other Sources of Cash	————	————

TOTAL LIQUID INVESTMENTS ————

Illiquid Investments		
Annuities	————	————
Business Equity/Partnership Interest	————	————

Resource	Total Value/ Monthly Income	Rate of Return (Annual %)
Company Stock Options	————	————
ESOP/Company Stock	————	————
Company Defined-Benefit Plan	————	————
EE U.S. Savings Bonds	————	————
Certificates of Deposit	————	————
Deferred Compensation Plan	————	————
401(k)/403(b)	————	————
IRAs (Roths, Spousal, conventional)	————	————
Keogh/SEP-IRA/SAR-SEP, SIMPLE	————	————
Rental Real Estate Equity	————	————
Home Equity	————	————
Collectibles	————	————
Real Estate Partnerships	————	————
Private Placements	————	————
Preferred Stock/IPOs	————	————
Closely held (private) Company Stock	————	————

TOTAL LIQUID INVESTMENTS   ————

TOTAL ILLIQUID INVESTMENTS + ————

TOTAL ASSETS = ————

HOW MUCH WILL YOUR RETIREMENT INCOME STREAM BE?

Here's some easy math. Now that you know how much you have, pull out any projected monthly payments or "income streams" from the second column that you can predict now. Typically, they consist of:

1. Interest income from stock and bond dividends/interest   _____

2. Monthly company defined-benefit pension payments   _____

3. Annuity payments   _____

4. Real estate rental income   _____

5. Other sources of income   _____

6. Part-time work/consulting   _____

(A) TOTAL INITIAL MONTHLY PROJECTED INCOME   _____

Now figure out how much you will pull out of this income stream every year to cover your living expenses. If you know you'll have enough cash on hand (money not in tax-deferred accounts), then this exercise will apply to later years of retirement. If you have been able to live on a company defined-benefit monthly payment (and Social Security), then this exercise may not be necessary if your expenses are in line with your initial projected income. Withdrawals draw down your long-term funds, so the lower the withdrawal, the greater chance your money will be able to grow over time and provide for you in your old age. Remember, you may need this money in your ninth and tenth decades.

1. MULTIPLY A × .04 = CONSERVATIVE WITHDRAWAL   _____

2. MULTIPLY A × .05 = MODERATE WITHDRAWAL   _____

3. MULTIPLY A × .06 = LARGE WITHDRAWAL   _____

Your withdrawals are based on the amount of income you convert into a "stream" for your retirement. Calculate 1, 2, and 3 and compare with your Total Monthly Expenses (see page 26). If you're coming up short in your income stream, you'll either need to invest more or cut back your expenses. Ideally, you should be able to live on a 4% withdrawal rate. That is, you're taking out no more than 4% a year from your nest egg. This is not written in stone, however. Other factors to consider are rate of return on your assets (the higher the better), the risk you're taking to get that return, and the mix of investments (growth and income).

The No-Brainer Way to Structure an Income Stream

There's little doubt you can structure your income stream based on pulling money out of your present investments. If you don't want to do the work, you can buy a *single-premium immediate annuity.* This is a product that essentially hands your money back to you in equal monthly payments—and guarantees the income stream from five years to life.

Like most annuities, "immediates" are sold by insurance companies. That means they involve additional management, administration, mortality, and "surrender" charges (fees you pay if you withdraw money before a certain date). In other words, they cost several percentage points more than if you were to do it yourself. There are, however, some distinct advantages to using immediates in spite of this:

- **Immediate annuities pay right away.** The day you retire is the day your immediate annuity kicks in. No rollover period, no waiting for your pension, no more paperwork once you fill out an application.

- **They're flexible.** You can structure them to pay only you or for "joint and survivor." That means your spouse is covered if you should die, although the monthly payments are from 5 to 15 percent lower should that happen. You can even structure them to be *term certain* for only a fixed period of time—usually from five to twenty-five years. That may cover you until you are ready to withdraw other retirement funds.

■ **You can set them up with existing funds.** You can transfer money from other annuities or from "qualified" plans like 401 (k)s to set up an immediate.

■ **They have some tax advantages.** Unlike qualified plans where the entire distribution is a taxable event, only some of the annuity payment is taxable since you are receiving part of your principal back.

■ **You can build in growth.** Most immediate annuities are based on fixed-income investments, but you can purchase a variable annuity that allows you to invest in stock mutual funds. Although the fee structure is higher—and your total return will probably be lower than an index fund in another tax-deferred account—this is a viable option to grow your money.

■ **They are widely available.** Nearly every major life insurer sells immediate annuities and they are widely marketed on the Internet (see www.annuitychoice.com). Shop for the annuities with the lowest-possible cost structure and no surrender charges if you decide to change insurers. Also, choose a company with the highest Best's or Standard and Poor's financial rating. The higher the financial grade, the more likely that company will be in business thirty years from now.

So How Much Do I Have Now?

There's no shame in coming up short in this last section. Since we're building maximum flexibility into your new prosperity plan, you'll have the opportunity to "goose up" the numbers in several ways. As Dick Parker noted in the last chapter, you may not need as much as you think to retire early, especially if you anticipate that your mortgage will be paid off by the time you stop working full-time, you only have one vehicle, and you have no one outside of your significant other to support. Unless you're thinking of buying a house, a car, a boat, and going on a spending spree after you quit work, your cost of living will most likely go down quite a bit. That's where the "65% to 80%" of your pre-retirement income formula comes into play. Let's see where you stand now:

1. How much will you need to live on monthly, based on your total monthly expenses? For this question, you'll need to retrieve some numbers from step 2's Total Monthly Expenses on page 26. Subtract any adjustments through **prosperity plan savings** (we'll use this figure later) from your monthly spending total and that will be your . . .

MONTHLY PRE-RETIREMENT EXPENSES _____

2. Add Total Initial Monthly Projected Income (page 54) to any other projected monthly income from part-time employment or other income sources. This is your . . .

PROSPERITY PLAN INITIAL INCOME _____

3. If you qualify, add Social Security income. If you make under $25,000, enter $666; between $25,000 to $40,000, enter $1,000; over $40,000, enter $1,208. *Don't forget to figure in Social Security at a later date; you qualify starting at age 62! (It'll still be there for coming generations, trust me.)*

SOCIAL SECURITY INCOME _____

4. Add up other income

CASH ACCOUNTS, INHERITANCE, SALE OF ASSETS, ETC. _____

Add items 2 through 4. This is your . . .

PROSPERITY PLAN INCOME BENCHMARK _____

5. Now take your Prosperity Plan Income Benchmark

AND SUBTRACT YOUR (PRE-RETIREMENT) SALARY – _____

THIS IS YOUR . . . INITIAL RETIREMENT INCOME _____

What you've just done is prepare a thumbnail sketch of how much income you'll have in retirement. Your prosperity plan benchmark and initial retirement income numbers are rough estimates, though. We haven't added in projected investment income from vehicles like IRAs or 401(k)s or tapped into any of your non-employment retirement funds. I just want to show you how your income picture looks without a regular salary and show you how to create an income stream from your investments. Since you've already made adjustments in what you can cut out of your spending portrait, you have a much better idea about what you need to live on. We haven't finished yet, however. That's because we're now going to figure in some further prosperity plan adjustments.

The initial pre-retirement income figure is not *the* number you'll use as the monthly income amount you'll count on in retirement. We have a few more things to do, so don't put the calculator away quite yet. There are certain costs that will go away. Let's make some more adjustments to Total Monthly Expenses, so that you'll see how you'll need less income to cover your lifestyle costs. *And don't forget that you may have had prosperity savings from relocating, refinancing your mortgage, or reducing your transportation budget to consider here.*

NEW PROSPERITY TIP

The best way of tracking expenses is to save every receipt, bill, and checking account statement every month and add everything up by category. Keep all of your records in an expandable folder. For maximum flexibility in your reduced income future, store up enough money in your cash accounts to cover at least a year's worth of expenses (see step 8). That will give you more time to decide how much money to withdraw from your tax-deferred plans.

The following items are part of your overall monthly expenses when you work full-time that you won't have when you retire. Without your commute to work you won't be getting on a train or bus or incurring the expense of running another car five or six days a week. You most likely won't need business suits, regular hair care, or dry cleaning. You won't be doing any unreimbursed business travel or entertainment. You probably won't have kids in school (if you do, you'll need to read step 7). You'll even save a bundle by eating lunch at home (unless you were bringing in your lunch all these years, and for that, Bravo!). And you can cash in the life-insurance policy and stop paying premiums if your spouse is well taken care of by your retirement assets and you have no other dependents who would suffer if you weren't supporting them. So let's look at how you can save some more money.

MORE PROSPERITY PLAN SAVINGS

Item	Monthly Savings
Clothing	_____
Commuting Expenses	_____
Daily Lunches (unreimbursed)	_____
Dry Cleaning	_____
Health Club	_____
Tuition Bills (for your kids?)	_____
Personal Care Services (hair, spa, etc.)	_____
Unreimbursed Business Expenses	_____
Payroll Taxes	_____
Second/Third Vehicle	_____
Mortgage	_____
Life Insurance Premiums	_____
Miscellaneous	_____

TOTAL *EXTRA* PROSPERITY PLAN ADJUSTMENTS _____

These are savings that reduce your total post-retirement monthly expenses. To be fair, add in any additional costs that your employer is no longer footing the bill for, such as health care, travel, entertainment, and other items.

The benchmark, however, isn't a done deal as far as how much you need goes. Hang in there. Let's try one more stab at prosperity savings.

Coming Up Short? Use Home Equity
to Fuel Your Prosperity Plan

When you were told by bankers that your home was like a savings account, that statement was partially right and partially wrong. For most people in most areas, homes build equity, but the rate of return varies quite a bit. Unlike savings accounts, which are generally poor but liquid investments, your home is a store of value that's largely *illiquid.* It's complicated and costly getting the money out. First, there's the real estate sales commission when you sell it, unless you do a "for sale by owner" or FSBO (fizbo). That's a cool 6% that comes right off the top of your (probably reduced) selling price. Then there are the credit checks, surveys, home inspections, lawyer's fees, home warranties, repairs, and cosmetic fix-ups you cover before you sell. Can you imagine the rioting at banks if they charged 6% plus fees just to get at your money, which is probably earning only 4% to begin with? (Banks are actually charging up to $1.50 to withdraw money from automated-teller machines, but no burning-banker effigies sighted to date.)

The best thing you can hope for on the investment side of home equity is that you'll at least keep pace with the rate of inflation. So expect 2% to 3% nominal return (or roughly the consumer price index) on the money you put into your home. Don't expect that kind of return, however, on repairs like furnaces, windows, roofing, gutters, siding, electrical, plumbing, and other items that people aren't willing to pay extra for in any market. That's a fairly dependable figure because you're not taxed on the capital gain when you sell it—unless you clear more than $500,000 (per couple).

You come out ahead somewhat when you figure in the tax deductibility of your property taxes and even more if you're in an area of high demand for real estate and have a marketable property. In that case, you'll handily beat inflation. Unfortunately, most areas are not hot real estate markets most of the time, so you can't really count on a reliable rate of return. A house is not a bond. It won't pay you a fixed monthly income (unless you take out a "reverse mortgage" [designed for elderly people who can tap home equity for a monthly income] on the equity and want to forgo passing it on to your survivors).

For example, say you live in a town dominated by one factory or industry and the corporation decides to shut down or relocate the plant to Mexico or the Far East. You know what happens to your home value? *Kerplunk.* Or, say you happen to be fortunate to live in an area where they can't find enough people to fill the jobs. In that case, you can take that modest bungalow and turn it around in a day and have people bidding above your asking price. You're on the pig's back then.

When it comes to retirement planning, the major question is not "Do I want to keep paying a mortgage?" it's "Do I have enough to retire on?" There are three schools of thought on this one:

1. I'm paying off the mortgage and eliminating my biggest monthly payment. For most people, this is a great idea, provided you plan to stay put and you have enough money through your many sources of income and investments for your new prosperity plan. But if you pony up a significant amount of money (say $10,000 plus) to pay off the note, you could be missing an "opportunity cost." In other words, you're taking cash that could be making roughly 8% in the stock market to pay for an investment that's appreciating at 3% to 4% in average real estate markets. This is a difficult decision. If you're already comfortable on the investment side, however, this isn't such a bad idea. Paying off your mortgage reduces your monthly expenses, but be careful not to deplete your long-term investments to do it. If you'll feel more comfortable *without* a mortgage—and it will enhance your prosperity—then go ahead and make sure you can afford to do it. But don't pay it off with tax-deferred money from your retirement plan. Jim Platania, a certified financial planner I've known for years who's based in Mt. Prospect, Illinois, told me he had a client who dipped into 401 (k) funds to pay off a mortgage, a move he called "a financially devastating mistake." Not only was this client nailed with taxes (because he withdrew the money before age 59½ and was hit with a 10% tax), the withdrawal bumped him into a higher tax bracket, so he paid even more income taxes. Using your retirement money to pay off the mortgage can be a disaster because you can't make it up later on in retirement (unless you are expecting a windfall from another source). Once you spend the money, it stops working for you and you may run out of retirement funds much earlier than you had hoped.

2. I'm selling the house, buying a smaller home, and investing the difference. You can keep the gains tax-free as long as they are under $500,000 (for couples filing jointly; $250,000 for singles). Here's how this strategy would work: First you sell the family home. Let's say you live in a solid, metropolitan area and your house sells for $300,000, then you downsize to a condo that sells for $150,000 either near your present area or you relocate. Maybe you don't need four bedrooms and a basement anymore. Why pay the taxes and maintenance on unused space? Not only do you have $150,000 to invest at a higher rate of return in the stock market—let's say 10% vs. 4% on your real estate investment—you can create an income stream and add growth to your portfolio that will beat inflation over time. A bonus to this scenario is that you can also reduce your monthly expenses across the board. Taxes, utilities, maintenance, and repairs drop your income stream hundreds of dollars a month. This could be the difference between affording an early retirement and waiting for Social Security to kick in at sixty-five. If you can't emotionally deal with the prospect of leaving behind "all those memories," then this is not an option. For most homeowners, though, it's a viable source of funding for a new prosperity plan.

3. I'm keeping the mortgage, but refinancing it and taking out equity. If you really can't sell the family home and you have a low mortgage payment, this option also makes sense. Your home is not a great investment, but it has "equity-financing power." That is, you can leverage it to get money out of it. The big downside is that you'll actually increase the amount you'll need to pay off (you're going into more debt) and pay money to get at your money (closing costs). This is a last resort, but consider this: Although your home isn't a savings account, you can still get at the money. There's really nothing wrong with having a mortgage. If you do need to sell the house, at some point you can. *Voilà!* No more mortgage. And you won't be saddling your heirs with a debt, either, because they can turn around and sell the home, too, or keep it for the equity-financing power. You could also refinance and take out equity to pay cash for a second home. Then move to that second home when the time is right and sell the first home. Or, you could live in the second home part-time and keep the first. If you choose to relocate, for example, you can buy the second home and rent out the first home. Then, if you've decided to relocate permanently, you can sell the first home (and pay off the home-equity loan). Well, you get the picture. Just be careful that your payments on the loan aren't reducing your monthly income to the point that you are struggling to make ends meet. Home-equity funds aren't "found" dollars, because you still have to pay back the loan—with interest.

No matter which option you choose, you may need to make an adjustment to your total monthly expenses. If you save money by *not* having a mortgage or reducing your expenses, do the appropriate subtraction from your monthly expenses total now to arrive at a new prosperity adjustment (p. 59), which is how much you're spending every month for basic expenses minus any major changes such as selling your home. You'll subtract this from your total monthly expenses.

Here's the big question: Does your Prosperity Plan Income Benchmark (p. 57) cover your (adjusted) Total Monthly Expenses? In other words, do you have enough to support your lifestyle? You know how much you need to pay the bills every month. If you're still coming up short, delve into the next step and pay special attention to step 6. If your expenses don't exceed your

NEW PROSPERITY TIP

If you decide that it's in your best interest to pay off your mortgage early, you can do it over time by adding extra payments to your loan's principal. Every bank will allow you to do this, provided you note on the payment coupon the amount that is paid to "principal only." Otherwise you are paying interest—and principal. There's no limit on how aggressive you can be in paying off your loan early. On a 30-year $200,000 note at 7.25%, adding $200 a month will knock nearly ten years off the term of the loan. An extra $100 month will pare five years from the term.

income, proceed to step 5. Did you have any idea this would be as fun as playing Monopoly? The best part is that you'll collect far more than $200 when you pass Go.

This Is a Big One: Did You Plan for Health Care?

The one flaw in Don Kraft's retirement plan was forgetting to plan for the rising costs of health care (it's not a fatal mistake since he's on Medicare now), so let's go over this item carefully. After you determine if you'll have enough money to retire, you'll need to plan for your and your spouse's health care. With health-care costs rising at nearly double the rate of inflation, an acute illness or surgery can devastate your new prosperity plan if you don't have proper coverage. You *can't* assume that all of your health-care costs will be covered if you retire early, so here are the alternatives:

- Negotiate to pay for major medical coverage at the company's group rate when you retire. Most early-retirement packages worth their salt will cover the premiums anyway.

- If you are leaving a company, you are entitled by federal law to COBRA (Consolidated Omnibus Budget Reconciliation Act) health benefits for eighteen months. That means the company must offer the lower group-rate premium at 102% of their cost for that period of time. That's still a good deal for most people. After the year-and-a-half period, though, you're on your own and your health-care costs could easily double. You should definitely plan for this cost.

- Individual health plans are incredibly expensive, but you can shop around for the best deal. Do an Internet search of insurance brokers for the best rate (see step 8). Like most health policies, you'll get the best rate if you are healthy, not overweight, and don't have any preexisting conditions like heart disease, diabetes, and a long list of maladies. Since few people have spotless health records, you'll need to shop for the best rate by quoting dozens of insurers. One easy way of saving on premiums is to keep your deductibles high. You'll pay a lot less if your deductible—or out-of-pocket annual expense—is $1,000 or more, versus $250. Under a federal law known as "Kennedy-Kassenbaum," or the Health Insurance Portability and Accountability Act (HIPAA), insurers must still insure you if you have preexisting conditions, but they will find a way to gouge you on the premium.

- You can often find group coverage at reasonable rates through local chambers of commerce, professional associations, small-business groups, and alumni associations. See Resources at the end of this book for a list of organizations offering affordable coverage at group rates.

- Don't forget other health-care items that can be huge out-of-pocket expenses. Chances are you won't have dental insurance. If you're looking at several root canals or bridgework, your dentist's bill could be sizable. What about contacts and eyeglasses and the tests that typically accompany them? Do you need regular physical therapy, chiropractic, or mental health care? Is it covered by your post-retirement insurance or your former employer's continuing health plan? Until you qualify for Medicare, you have to do some honest accounting of your total health-care out-of-pocket expenses.

- In addition to a comprehensive health plan, I strongly suggest you have a *wellness* plan, too. This really doesn't cost you much of anything. Most hospitals and modern clinics offer this service, but you'll probably pay for the physicals and tests it calls for out of pocket, unless you find an unusually generous managed-care plan. *Wellness* refers to health maintenance; that is, keeping you well by doing the things that promote health and prevent disease. The first step of a wellness plan is a comprehensive checkup that scans all of your vital systems—heart, respiratory, liver, blood, muscular-skeletal. This report gives you a heads-up on things to keep an eye on. For example, if you have high blood pressure, it's highly treatable with medication, which may prevent a stroke down the road. If your blood sugar is too high, you may be able to control that with diet. A well-conceived wellness plan integrates what is known about your medical history, new information from a thorough checkup and tests, and a comprehensive plan of medication (if needed), exercise, diet, and other activities. If you are leaving the workforce and want to stay healthy, a wellness plan is a reasonable vehicle to *keep* you healthy and should be a linchpin of every new prosperity plan.

What If You're Getting Out Now: Evaluating Early-Retirement Plans

The life you want may be attainable in a short period of time if your employer is offering you some incentives to leave now. But consider these buyout plans carefully. Not everyone who is offered a buyout can afford to retire. You'll still need to see if your spending is out of balance with your income and whether your investment/ pension income will be enough to comfortably sustain your household. Don Kraft, for example, already had an explicit portrait of his expenses and investment returns before he left IBM. You should prepare in the same way.

Gordon Medlock, Ph.D., who counsels early retirees as part of his position with the John Joseph Group, a Chicago-based out-placement firm, notes that the single biggest barrier for early retirees is that they are not financially secure enough to leave the workforce, often even when they are offered generous buyouts. "Not having enough money is the most common pitfall [for them]," Medlock says.

That's why it's important to take a step back and determine whether the combination of investment and pension income will allow you to sustain your lifestyle after full-time work. Remember, when faced with a buyout package, you can also consider lifestyle changes through prosperity savings. That might tip the balance in your favor. If you are an empty-nester, for example, you could sell your home, buy a smaller place, and put the equity into your retirement fund or convert it into an income stream, as we've looked at in this chapter. Or you could cash in on those extra prosperity savings by eliminating one vehicle, commuting costs, and all the other expenses connected with going to work to make a new prosperity plan possible.

You could also reach the conclusion after running the numbers that you need to continue working for a while and contribute more to your retirement plans. Here's how to discern what to do when your employer dangles that big carrot of leaving your full-time employment with a generous package:

- **What is the total package?** Obtain a written commitment as to what the plan will include, when it pays out, and for how long. If you need details, ask. If you want more, see if the package is negotiable. Sometimes you can obtain more health-care coverage or a bigger payout than your employer's original offer. You are saving the company money by leaving, so they should do their best to accommodate you.

- **How much health care is included?** The best deals will cover you until you qualify for Medicare. Even better deals cover most of your out-of-pocket expenses like dental and eye-care with the same benefits you had while working. The less generous packages cover your health-care premiums for a set period such as two years, then allow you to pay for your coverage at a group rate. Health care is the second most important component of your buyout plan. You can't make a decision until you know how much you're going to pay out of pocket and for how long.

- **Is this the final offer?** It's not unusual for corporate "reductions in force" to happen in waves. Depending on the company you work for, these waves of layoffs may produce more generous buyouts— or they may not. When companies have to trim their bottom line by cutting the workforce, they've already done the math on how much money they'll be saving by buying you out. If you're with a company that's had a history of cutbacks, ask those who've taken the packages in earlier waves what they got, then compare that with what you're being offered. If you know your position won't be eliminated, you may even stay on (if you're reasonably sure you won't be fired later). If the company does buyouts in rounds, you may get a better deal later on, but there's clearly a risk that you may not.

- **Can I leave gradually?** You may not have to leave cold turkey—that is, quit entirely and never return, which can be difficult for most workers to do—unless you really hate your employer or job. It may be possible for you to negotiate reductions in the hours you work—and still get full benefits or at least have your health insurance covered. A lot of corporations may need to cut their full-time workforce but are smart enough to realize they can't replace your expertise or experience very easily. In that situation, they may offer you a consultancy contract, which you negotiate. You can then work from home, set your own hours, and make a pretty good income, although you won't be on salary anymore and won't have the full benefits package. This could be a less stressful transition from full- to part-time work, if this is something you can work out.

- **Could I be hired back?** Some companies lay off more people than they need to or make reductions due to short-term or seasonal changes in the markets for what they sell. If you work for such a company—particularly those in "cyclical" businesses—you may be able to return, especially if your position is not being phased out and your expertise is needed. Although corporate loyalty isn't what it used to be, managers have long memories for employees who are productive and save the corporation money through their diligence and knowledge. If you can't afford to quit now, keep in mind that the longer you work, the more you can save. Just keep in mind that most reductions in force these days are due to smaller markets, automation, or cost-cutting, which doesn't ensure that your job description will even exist in the future.

- **How much will I get if I go?** This is the most complicated part, but one that is the single most important element. How much severance will you receive? Every company has its own formula, but the more severance you get, the better. Severance is like a bonus for walking out the door quietly and it is often negotiable, depending on how high up you are on the management chain. What percentage of your salary will you receive and for how long? The most generous plans will pay you for a few years after you leave; the least generous pay just a few months. What are the fringes? It's not unusual for top-drawer buyouts to include financial planning, retirement counseling, and even money for tuition or retraining. What is the value of these benefits and services? Total everything up and check again whether the package will cover your financial needs (adjusted to include *your* prosperity savings). At the very least, you should be able to cover at least a year of living expenses with funds from your buyout package or cash you have in short-term (liquid) savings, money market accounts, CDs, or other vehicles. This will give you time to determine what your true post-retirement expenses are like and how to adjust accordingly.

Pulling Money Out of Tax-Deferred Plans If You're Under 59½

If you don't have that salary coming in, you'll need a monthly income stream from your retirement plans. As we've looked at in earlier chapters, this money comes from three sources: (1) Your liquid assets, such as money market accounts, non-tax-deferred savings, and other sources, which you've figured out earlier in this chapter; (2) your investments; and (3) your early-retirement buyout (if you got one). You should already have a clear picture of how much you have socked away in liquid assets and investments, so you need to focus on how to direct the money from those investments into a tax-efficient income stream.

If you are 59½ or older, the only tax consequences of withdrawing money from your tax-deferred accounts is paying income tax. It's unlikely that withdrawing this money will bump you into a higher bracket, and often you're in a lower bracket when you retire. Ideally, you won't have to tap into your tax-deferred money until at least a year or more into retirement. As I mentioned in step 2, you'll need at least a year to get a clear view of your actual spending portrait.

The IRS has a neat rule called the 72(t) exemption that allows you to pull out funds from your tax-deferred plans before 59½. The key to understanding this rule—like all IRS regulations—is that there are other rules to follow before you can take advantage of

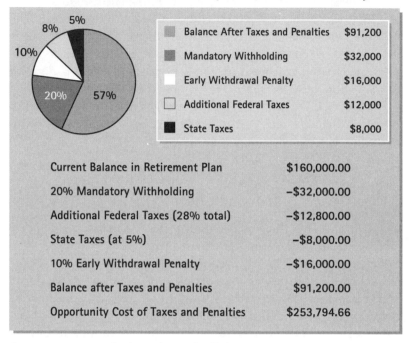

WHAT HAPPENS IF YOU TAKE YOUR LUMP-SUM BUYOUT AS CASH: THE NASTY TAX CONSEQUENCES (FOR A $160,000 LUMP SUM)

Balance After Taxes and Penalties	$91,200
Mandatory Withholding	$32,000
Early Withdrawal Penalty	$16,000
Additional Federal Taxes	$12,000
State Taxes	$8,000

Current Balance in Retirement Plan	$160,000.00
20% Mandatory Withholding	−$32,000.00
Additional Federal Taxes (28% total)	−$12,800.00
State Taxes (at 5%)	−$8,000.00
10% Early Withdrawal Penalty	−$16,000.00
Balance after Taxes and Penalties	$91,200.00
Opportunity Cost of Taxes and Penalties	$253,794.66

Source: www.strong-funds.com/strong/perl/rollover.pl

this special tax ruling. This exemption is formally known as the IRS Code Section 72 (t) (2) (a) (iv) and IRS Cumulative Bulletin Notice 89-25. To make it work, you can pull out your money without getting nicked by the 10% early-withdrawal penalty if you take your money out in "substantially equal periodic payments." Financial planners call this process "annuitization." It simply means you take out the same amount every month based on a preset withdrawal schedule. Here are the rules:

1. Once you decide to take the 72 (t), you are locked into that payment schedule for at least five years or until you hit 59½, whichever comes first.

2. To figure out how much your monthly payment will be, the IRS gives you three choices: (a) the *life expectancy* method, (b) the *amortization* method, and (c) the *annuity factor* method. Each method is based on equally dividing your funds, taking into account how long the IRS expects you to live.

3. Each method has its merits. You can calculate the payments yourself or hire an accountant or financial planner to wade through the arcane and dense language of IRS Publication 590. John Greaney, Webmaster of the Retire Early Home Page (www. geocities.com/wallstreet/8257) and early retiree extraordinaire featured in step 8, has boiled down the advantages and disadvantages in this handy table:

EARLY WITHDRAWAL METHODS: COMPARISONS

	Life Expectancy	Amor- tization	Annuity Factor
Optimal Retiree Age	Age 30 to 50	Age 50 to 59	Age 55 to 59
Size of Annual Withdrawal	Small	Large	Largest
Recalculate Annually	Yes	No	No
Outliving Assets Possible?*	Unlikely	Yes	Yes
Difficult to Calculate?	No	Maybe	Yes

Source: Retire Early Home Page

*The chance that you will spend all of your retirement funds in your lifetime.

Which method you choose is ultimately a function of how much you need the maximum monthly payment to be and how much work you want to go through to figure it out (or how much you want to pay someone else to do the calculations). As you can tell from the table, the life expectancy method is simplest because the IRS provides "mortality tables"—or guesses—on how long they think you're going to live given your present age. This method may, however, provide the smallest monthly payment because it is conservative and requires you to refigure it every year. The second and third methods will boost your monthly income, but that means using up more of your money and facing the possibility your money won't last your entire lifetime—especially if you are graced with a tenth decade.

Also keep in mind that if you're at least fifty-five, you may not even have to fool with weighing the three withdrawal methods. The IRS will let you pull out money without penalty if you "annuitize" in equal monthly payments. Once you know how much your income stream from your investments is going to be, you can ask the vital question we will explore next.

Will You Have Enough?
Some Serious Number Crunching

You now need to figure out how long your money will last. Since you know how much you have—or will receive from a buyout— then you'll need to tap into a number of resources that are best done on a computer (there's more on this subject in step 8). Basically, you'll need to project the future value of your total retirement assets based on:

1. **Average rate of return.** Go back to your list of assets and the rates of return you listed on pages 51–53 and average them. Here's a powerful rule of thumb: If your average rate of return is less than 7%, you're going to be tapping into principal sooner than you want to and your money may not last as long as you do. That's because your money may not be growing to beat the yearly ravages of inflation. This means your $10,000 (that's not outpacing inflation) will be worth $9,600 next year, $9,216 the following year—well, you get the picture. That means you should:

2. **Figure a *real* rate of return.** This is the actual rate of return, also known as the rate of return *minus* inflation, taxes, and management fees (see step 6 on how to beat that bugaboo). To calculate this, you'll need some software, which, unfortunately isn't built into this book. You can get some fairly reliable calculations on the Internet through a number of commercial Web sites. Try www.quicken.com, www.financenter.com, www.fidelity.com, www.troweprice.com, www.strong.com, and www.vanguard.com. The last four sites are sponsored by mutual fund houses, so they might want to help you out with your retirement funds. Quicken, T. Rowe Price, and Vanguard also have excellent software that you can use to make much more detailed projections.

3. **Is your rate of return sustainable?** That is, is it realistic and still growing your principal? If you're only earning 5%, for example, your *real* return after inflation, taxes, and fees could be in the red. On the other hand, it's unrealistic to think you can rack up more than 12% return a year. Most financial planners say 8% to 10% is doable and will easily outpace inflation over long periods of time. Remember, the long-term average for inflation throughout most of the twentieth century has been about 4%. But that's just an average. It's been as high as 14% and as low as 1%. If you figure on an inflation rate of 5%, you'll probably be playing it safe. Another factor you'll need to eye is how much you're withdrawing every year. The most solid guideline is not to touch your principal. As I mentioned earlier, a comfortable rule of thumb for withdrawing your

NEW PROSPERITY TIP

According to the Retire Early Home Page (www.geocities.com/wallstreet/8257), for a comfortable and sustainable retirement you'll need $200,000 to $250,000 in retirement funds for every $10,000 in annual pre-retirement income. That means a $1 million nest egg will support a $35,000 to $50,000 per year lifestyle at 8% rate of return until age ninety. A $500,000 kitty could support a retirement income of $20,000 to $25,000. You can, of course, make adjustments (as I've noted earlier in this chapter) so that you need less money to live on, which means starting out with a smaller nest egg.

tax-deferred funds is 4% a year—provided you are handily beating inflation in your real rate of return

4. **Are you getting enough growth?** You certainly won't be if your prosperity portfolio consists mostly of income investments, which don't beat inflation. That means a high percentage (at least 60%) of stocks and stock mutual funds. More on that in the next chapter.

Whew! What Was That All About Anyway?

1. Make sure you have a good portrait of your spending before you proceed to tally your investments. If you're not saving and investing, you can't move into a workable new prosperity plan. Don't forget to include health-care costs. Add in any extra prosperity savings.

2. Tally your sources of income combined with investments. Estimate an annual rate of return and project at present rates. Figure the real rate of return that subtracts inflation, taxes, and fees. Be conservative.

3. Project what your prosperity portfolio will look like given the real rate of return. Will it be enough? Do you have enough growth working for you?

4. If you can—or are forced—to leave the workforce before age sixty-two, figure out how to withdraw your funds from tax-deferred accounts. Evaluate early-retirement buyouts carefully.

5. If you're coming up short on rate of return or amount of funds needed to fund your prosperity portfolio, consider vehicles that will help get you there (see step 4).

Choosing and Setting Up Your New Prosperity Plan

There are three faithful friends—an old wife, an old dog, and ready money.

—Benjamin Franklin

When you change course in midstream, you better have a good rudder. Sue Stevens has always set her eye on a point on the horizon, has a good sense of direction, and has done what she needed to do to get there. As a successful cellist for fifteen years, she played with some of the finest ensembles in the country including the Chicago Symphony Orchestra and Lyric Opera Orchestra. Since her father was a big-band musician, being a professional musician was in her genes.

One day, though, Sue realized "other parts of my brain needed an outlet," so she embarked on a brave adventure and did something completely different at age thirty-three. While still working as a musician, she studied finance, earning an MBA from the prestigious University of Chicago Graduate School of Business, became a certified public accountant, a certified financial planner, a chartered financial analyst, and earned a master's degree in financial planning. While Sue can make more money as a financial planner, she was leaving an already lucrative career. Money wasn't necessarily the overriding issue in her case; she wanted to help people with their financial lives.

After working as a financial planning manager at Arthur Anderson in Chicago and as head of research and development at Vanguard Group in suburban Philadelphia, she came back to Chicago to work at Morningstar, a leading provider of mutual fund, stock, and variable insurance information.

Sue took a "virtual retirement." She left one full-time livelihood, music, and had the courage to learn and choose another. Although forty years ago such a transition would be unheard of, it is increasingly practiced. Sue sees the change as a way of balancing her life and work.

Because she had saved and invested in the right vehicles, Sue had the money to do something creative and challenging yet totally unrelated to what she had been doing. As a financial planner, she's working with Morningstar to build better financial-planning tools while starting her own financial-planning practice.

Although Sue's not talking about retirement herself yet, she's articulate about what you need to do in terms of "negotiating your lifestyle" and laying the groundwork for life and career changes. She suggests anyone considering early retirement should "break down into little pieces" these particulars of new prosperity planning:

- Review your company-retirement plans. What kinds of plans are they? Are they defined-benefit plans that pay fixed monthly amounts at retirement? Or are they defined-contribution plans in which you choose your investments and method of withdrawal?

- Understand your income stream before you retire. Where is the money coming from? A diverse income stream is best—one that combines non-tax-deferred savings with tax-deferred withdrawals.

- Do you know how to invest your retirement funds, especially if you are in defined-contribution plans and have other retirement vehicles not tied in to your company? You can educate yourself with books and free information on the Internet (see Resources at the end of this book). What do you need to know that you don't know now? Get the answers to these questions from those who've retired, or visit your local library and do some homework.

- Do you have a sufficient amount of "cushion" cash in short-term accounts such as money market funds? You may have unexpected expenses with your new lifestyle and you may need it for emergencies as well.

- What percentage of your portfolio is in stocks and bonds? Do you understand the risks of owning each class of investment and how they perform over time?

- Do you have an accurate picture of how much income you need (refer back to the previous two steps)?

- Can you do it on your own or do you need help? If you need professional advice, turn to a fee-only certified financial planner (see Resources).

There are two ways of approaching retirement plans. Either you have one through your employer and you've been diligent about fully funding it or you are vaguely aware they exist and uninformed about the full range of options or how they work. This chapter combines a primer on retirement plans—if you don't have one or understand them—and a fine-tuning section on getting the best possible return from what you have.

If your first reaction to this chapter is: "But my employer doesn't offer me *any* pension plan (or you're self-employed)," a panoply of plans are available. They are offered through banks, brokerage firms, insurers, mutual fund houses, and anybody who sells financial services and products. You can have a fully funded plan regardless of whether or not your employer offers one.

Definitions of pension plans and retirement vehicles are constantly changing. A pension forty years ago meant a fixed, monthly

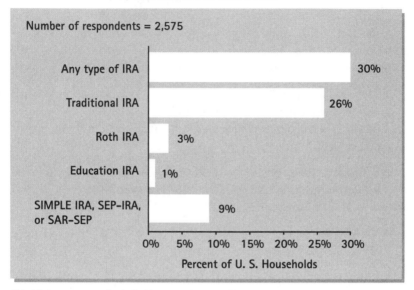

OWNERSHIP OF TYPES OF IRAs, 1998*
(Percent of U.S. households)

Number of respondents = 2,575

Any type of IRA	30%
Traditional IRA	26%
Roth IRA	3%
Education IRA	1%
SIMPLE IRA, SEP-IRA, or SAR-SEP	9%

Percent of U. S. Households

*Multiple responses included because households can own more than one type of IRA.
Source: Investment Company Institute

"defined benefit." You became entitled to one, or vested, usually after working only twenty years. You couldn't touch the money at any time, and if you left your employer (except for retirement), the money wouldn't travel with you. Although employers today aren't offering new defined-benefit plans—they are phasing them out—a monthly check was guaranteed (and federally insured by the Pension Benefit Guaranty Corporation) for the rest of your life. Today's "defined contribution" plans don't guarantee a dime and you have to manage your own money through a host of private mutual fund managers. One key benefit of a defined-contribution plan like a 401(k) or SEP-IRA is that you can take every dime with you at any time. Once you contribute, you are fully vested. The key to managing your own money, however, is choosing the right fund for the best possible return. Sue Stevens, for example, relies heavily on growth-stock index funds to fuel her retirement.

Once you choose the right vehicles (assuming you haven't done so already), you'll need to choose the right kinds of investments for your new prosperity portfolio. Like Sue Stevens, who was essentially a freelancer (self-employed), you can craft your own plans if you don't have one. Let's look at what you need to know and how to best use those investments:

Traditional Individual Retirement Account (IRA). Now a fixture in most individual retirement plans, an IRA is easy to set up, maintain, and fund. But the IRA, like most other retirement vehicles, is only a shell. You can fund it with stocks, bonds, mutual funds, and any other financial instrument outside of real estate. Since the IRS doesn't care who manages it, you can choose banks, mutual funds, brokerage houses, or "financial supermarkets." Typically you'll pay an annual IRA "custodian" fee of $10 in addition to management expenses. The idea here is to keep your expenses as low as possible and get as much return as you can.

Who Qualifies. Anyone with deferred income can contribute. There are "regular" and "spousal" IRAs. The regular forms are for individuals with earned income. "Spousal" IRAs are for married couples where only one spouse has earned income.

Contributions. You can deposit up to $2,000 per person per year. You can take a deduction for the contribution if your household income is less than $60,000 per year (filing jointly) or $40,000 for singles. If your spouse makes less than $150,000 per year, the other spouse can take the deduction.

Important Rules. You can withdraw the funds without penalty once you reach 59½ (and must withdraw the money at 70½), although you'll still pay income tax on the withdrawals (except if you apply the 72 (t) exemption, noted in the previous chapter). You are permitted penalty-free withdrawals to pay for higher-education expenses and first-time home purchases. But you still have to pay income tax on that money.

Roth IRA. Named after its proponent, Senator William Roth (R-Del.), the Roth IRA is a flexible vehicle that every investor should have. It's the same thing as a conventional IRA, only you can't take a deduction for it and—here's the good part—you can withdraw the funds *tax-free* once you hit 59½. The government doesn't even care what you use the money for, so you can use it for non-retirement purposes like paying college tuition bills (given my age and my daughter's likelihood of being in college when I'm sixty, this is a real possibility for me). You can also keep contributing to it no matter what your age and are not required to withdraw the funds at 70½, as you must with the conventional IRA.

Who Qualifies. Joint filers who make less than $150,000 in household annual income and single filers with less than $95,000 in income.

Contributions. You're allowed $2,000 per person per year if you meet the income guidelines above.

Important Rules. You must leave the funds in a Roth for at least five years before a withdrawal. Tax-free distributions are permitted if (1) you're 59½ or older; (2) the owner is disabled or deceased; (3) the owner is making a first-time home purchase. Distributions are only required upon death.

Education IRA. Although not a retirement vehicle, I mention this IRA because it will make your retirement easier if you have another tax-deferred vehicle in which to save for higher-education expenses. Despite the relative lack of generosity for this vehicle, it's worth having since any funds growing tax-deferred over time can compound significantly (see table below).

Who Qualifies. Like the Roth, you're not eligible if you make more than $150,000 a year and file jointly or more than $95,000 filing as a single.

Contributions. Only $500 per child per year.

Important Rules. Like the Roth, you're not permitted a tax deduction for this vehicle, and you can contribute only up to $500 per year per beneficiary (the child you hope to send to college). If the contributed funds *exceed* the cost of college, then you have to pay a 10% penalty and income tax. Contributions may not be made after the beneficiary reaches eighteen.

HOW MUCH WILL AN EDUCATION IRA BE WORTH?

Age of Child	Year-End Value
Birth	$540
5	$3,961
10	$8,989
15	$16,375
18	$22,381

NOTE: Projections assume an 8% annual rate of return (an average return for stocks over the past fifty years) and $500 contributions per year.

Simplified Employee Pension (SEP-IRA). If you are self-employed or are a small employer, this plan is a snap. This "simplified employee pension" is essentially an IRA for small business people. The contributions are tax deductible and are easy to set up because there is not much paperwork (a few pages at most).

Who Qualifies. Anyone in a company who earns a salary in any given year, although only employers can make contributions.

Contributions. Employers contribute up to 15% of each employee's yearly compensation (pretax) up to $24,000. (If you are self-employed, you make the contribution.)

Important Rules. You can decide how much to pay and when to contribute. It's usually managed by a mutual fund, which will provide the setup documents. There are no reporting documents for the IRS. Like conventional IRAs, the age 59½ rule applies and employees must start taking withdrawals at age 70½. If employees leave the company, however, the money is theirs to keep and they are free to change the fund manager. SEPs can be set up by corporations, sole proprietorships, partnerships, and "subchapter S" corporations (which pay your business taxes on your 1040). Employer's contributions are not counted as income for tax purposes.

SAR-SEP. A salary-reduction SEP-IRA was open to businesses with fewer than twenty-five employees. Contributions were made by the employer and employee. While less generous than SEP-IRAs, contributions were still pretax and earnings grew tax-deferred.

Who Qualifies. A regular employee earning a salary in a company with less than twenty-five workers.

Contributions. Employee contributions were capped at $9,500, although total contributions (employer and employee) couldn't exceed $24,000 in any given year.

Important Rules. New SAR-SEP IRAs couldn't be established after December 31, 1996, but if you have one, it's still a worthy vehicle. They were replaced by SIMPLE plans. At least 50 percent of a company's employees must be covered under the plan.

SIMPLE Plans. Also targeted for small businesses, SIMPLEs (Savings Incentive Match Plans) are also known as "mini-401 (k)s" because they are similar in design and provide for matching employer contributions. Although the setup is much more involved than a SEP, SIMPLEs offer much more in the way of flexibility.

Who Qualifies. Any regular employee earning a salary with a firm with less than 100 employees.

Contributions. Employees can contribute up to $6,000 per calendar year into a SIMPLE and may receive a matching contribution of up to 3% of their pay.

Important Rules. All contributions made to a SIMPLE are fully vested; that is, every dollar belongs to the employee the day he or she contributes it. Although the employer typically chooses the financial institution that will manage the funds, the employee is allowed to choose among different fund choices. Employees can transfer to another SIMPLE at another financial institution without cost or penalty. There's more paperwork involved because the trustee or manager of the funds must report the SIMPLE transactions to the IRS.

401(k) and 403(b). As one of the greatest success stories in retirement planning, these vehicles are the hallmarks of early-retirement programs. They are essentially the same, except that the 401(k) is offered by a for-profit employer and the 403 (b) is offered by a not-for-profit employer. Like SIMPLEs, they permit employers to match employee contributions.

Who Qualifies. Regular employees of for-profit (401[k]) or nonprofit (403[b]) organizations.

Contributions. You can contribute up to 11% of your pretax salary or $10,000.

Important Rules. Like every other retirement vehicle, the government doesn't want you touching your money until you are 59½ or you are permanently disabled or buying your first home. You'll have a wide range of mutual funds to choose from, the ability to switch from fund to fund, and various ways of tracking the funds, including the Internet and automated telephone services. Your company can match your contribution, which is "found" money you didn't have to work for. It's a classic profit-sharing plan with varying matches from 1% to 6%. Any pretax contributions to your 401(k) or 403(b) are exempt from federal income tax withholding, although your company must pay FICA or Social Security and Medicare taxes. The bells and whistles a 401(k) offers allow you to take out loans against your money, choose from a variety of independent mutual fund managers, and check your balance at any time.

Keogh Self-Employed Plan. An older, more flexible version of the 401(k), Keogh plans have been set up for years by smaller businesses. The same rules that apply to IRAs apply to Keoghs, only Keoghs give employers more options on how to contribute to employees' pensions. There are also more rules and paperwork.

Who Qualifies. Self-employed persons or partners, including sole proprietors filing Schedule C and partners filing Schedule E.

Contributions. Up to $30,000 per year or 13.4% of income for profit-sharing and defined-benefit plans; 20% of yearly income up to $30,000 for money-purchase plans.

Important Rules. The employer may offer a *money-purchase, profit-sharing,* or *defined-benefit plan,* but the rules are fairly well defined for each and you need an accountant to help set one up.

- If it's a profit-sharing plan, the employer must match a fixed-percentage contribution.

- Money-purchase plans permit larger contributions, but those contributions are mandatory fixed percentages each year no matter how much profit the company makes.

- Defined-benefit plans are traditional pensions that pay a fixed amount at retirement and the employee has no control over how the money's managed.

All contributions are pretax and subject to the same withdrawal rules as IRAs.

Other Kinds of Investment Vehicles

Certain vehicles deserve a separate discussion because they are generally not offered by all employers and need to be considered carefully. Annuities, for example, are to be bought only if you've invested in all other possible forms of pretax and tax-deferred plans because they are funded with after-tax money and may carry high management and administration charges. Employee stock ownership plan (ESOP) rules tend to be complicated and involve buying company (your employer's only) stock at a discount. Keep in mind that, like any investment, you should avoid concentrating all of your holdings in one vehicle. Nonqualified plans are usually only available to highly compensated employees. If you're fortunate enough to have one, then consult a financial planner or accountant on withdrawing money from it to avoid tax problems.

Annuities. These are tax-deferred vehicles typically offered by an insurance company. After age 59½, you can annuitize a monthly payment. You can't deduct the contributions, and the payments are subject to ordinary income tax. *Variable* annuities offer you a selection of mutual funds that permit you to boost your return (usually through stock funds). The management and administrative fees on these vehicles zap your total return to such an extent that it's better to invest in a low-cost mutual fund (particularly an index fund) within an IRA or similar vehicle. There are also annuities within pension plans, which are called "qualified" annuities. The same rules apply.

ESOPs. Employee stock ownership plans are among the oldest forms of retirement vehicles and can be excellent because they allow employees the option to purchase company stock at a discount on a regular basis. You can "buy low and sell high" with your company's stock and do fairly well. It's a bad idea, however, to have most of your retirement dollars in an ESOP since you'll be increasing your investment risk if something happens to your company's bottom line. Some employers even offer a cash incentive to their stock bonus plans; that is, they'll help you buy the stock. This is not something a small business can set up easily.

Nonqualified Plans. Since no independent trustee is involved (and the plans may not have to be approved by the IRS), the employer has a lot more freedom to offer these to any employee, usually highly compensated managers or executives. They take the form of stock, stock options, or deferred cash bonuses—a real plus if you qualify. These plans generally involve deferring income until a later date. An employer will set up a plan that will pay you a bonus ten years from now, for example. One of the big problems of nonqualified plans is that if your business runs into financial trouble, the money in the deferred plan may be used to pay business debts.

> **NEW PROSPERITY TIP**
>
> To land new business, some brokerage houses and mutual fund firms will waive their annual custodial fee (it usually ranges from $10 to $15 a year). You may be able to get the fee waived simply by asking—the financial services industry is a competitive business. Also, don't forget that even if you pay the fees, they are deductible from your taxes if you itemize them on Form 1040, Schedule A.

Are You Getting the Best Possible Return from Your Retirement Vehicles?

Most investors don't realize that one of the biggest drains on their investment dollars are the middlemen managing them. You can't control how much your company pays in management fees—although you can certainly complain about it. For vehicles you set up yourself, look for stock funds that charge less than 0.50% per year in expenses (also known as the expense ratio). The lower the fees, the more your total return. Say you have a $100,000 balance in an IRA and you're in a stock fund that charges you 1.5% a year to manage it. I know that doesn't sound like a lot, but over twenty years, the manager will have walked away with $30,000 of your money. In a stock fund with an 0.50% expense ratio, the manager gets only $10,000—a third as much. It all adds up over time. Broker- and bank-sold funds and funds within variable annuities are even costlier to manage because there are more middlemen to compensate. Avoid them.

Since most of our discussion on investing for growth focuses on stock mutual funds, you need to know the variety of funds you can invest in. That means you should also educate yourself about the dozens of variations of stock funds and diversify among them. While large U.S. companies have been the dominant players in the market for the past decade, that won't always be the case. Consider small- or mid-sized companies or firms based overseas (see the following portfolios). Besides, by diversifying into other markets, you'll be lowering your overall risk. Since you have a choice of a wide variety of funds (there are more than six thousand of them), here are some suggested allocations:

NEW PROSPERITY PORTFOLIOS

Dominant Domestic Allocation

40% U.S. Large-Capitalization Stocks

20% U.S. Small-Cap Stocks

20% International Stocks

20% U.S. Corporate or Government Bonds (Income)

More Diversification, Less Risk

20% U.S. Large-Cap Stocks

20% U.S. Mid-Cap Stocks

20% Small-Cap Stocks

20% International Stocks

20% U.S. Corporate Bonds

Contrarian Mix, Higher Risk

40% U.S. Small-Cap Stocks

20% U.S. Large-Cap Stocks

20% U.S. "Value" Stocks*

20% International Stocks

* A value stock is one that is bought at a discount to book value.

Are You Contributing as Much as You Possibly Can?

You'll need to put every dollar possible into your retirement fund if you want to retire early. "Max out" your company profit-sharing plans first by contributing the maximum from your salary because *pretax* dollars are working hardest for you inside a tax-deferred vehicle. Then take *after-tax* dollars and hit the limit on your IRAs, starting with a Roth. Can you contribute to a 401(k), a Roth, and a conventional IRA? Yes, as long as you don't exceed the income limits ($150,000 in yearly income for married couples filing jointly; $95,000 for singles). You can even have a business on the side, fund your SEP or SIMPLE IRA, and still contribute to the other vehicles. If you do this, you'll see that the utter magic of tax-deferred compounding will work wonders over time. It's like someone giving you a 15% to 28% bonus for investing your money. Look at these numbers:

THE MIRACLE OF TAX-DEFERRED COMPOUNDING

$1,000 Initial Investment at 8% annual return, 28% tax bracket

Value at End of . . .	Taxable Account	Tax-Deferred After-tax	Tax-Deferred Pretax
5 years	$953	$1,058	$1,469
10 years	$1,261	$1,554	$2,159
20 years	$2,207	$3,356	$4,661
30 years	$3,863	$7,245	$10,063
40 years	$6,764	$15,642	$21,725

As you can see, the taxable account produces the poorest total return over time. You can do better with a tax-deferred vehicle funded with after-tax dollars such as a nondeductible IRA, but the best deal is a tax-deferred plan funded with pretax dollars such as a 401(k) profit-sharing plan. Keep in mind that your initial investment with the first two plans is $720 after taxes, so $280 keeps coming out of your total return year after year. Of course, it's a good idea to fund all of your retirement vehicles; just make sure your first dollars go into the pretax-funded vehicle. In terms of nominal annual return, you'll do nearly four times as well.

Should I Borrow from My 401(k)?

The option of borrowing from your 401(k) can certainly sound appealing, but resist it. Most large plans permit you to borrow money and pay it back to yourself at the prime rate or some other predetermined rate. There are two catches: (1) you'll have to pay the balance back in full if you leave the employment of that company, and (2) there's that nasty opportunity cost of lost returns that can never be recovered. If you want to seed your new prosperity plan, this is like pouring herbicide all over it. If you really need the money when a catastrophe strikes, certain "hardship" withdrawals are permitted, but you'll probably pay tax on the funds and get hit with a 10% penalty if the hardship doesn't meet the plan's strict rules. As I mentioned earlier, don't even think of tapping the funds to pay off a mortgage. Tapping this money will set you back for the rest of your life because you won't have the time to earn it back and still have it grow and compound in a tax-deferred account, and you'll also have to pay back the loan in full when you leave your employer—or get socked with taxes.

New Prosperity Vehicles:
What You Need to Know

1. If you don't have a retirement plan, get one and fully fund it.

■

2. Know the differences between the various kinds of plans and choose the one that suits your needs. Set one up and choose low-cost mutual funds to fund them.

■

3. Understand the rules of each plan and choose fund managers who offer you the most service for the lowest cost. Diversify between types of funds.

4. Don't borrow from your 401(k).

Creating Your Own Private Utopia

*Fame or Integrity: which is more important? Money or happiness:
which is more valuable? Success or failure: which is more destructive? If
you look to others for fulfillment, you will never be truly fulfilled. If
your happiness depends on money, you will never be happy with
yourself. Be content with what you have; rejoice in the way things are.
When you realize there is nothing lacking, the whole world belongs
to you.*

—Tao Te Ching

Pat Gaughan has translated his success in the workplace into his
passion for helping others, although like most life journeys, his had
a number of switchbacks. After graduating from St. Patrick's High
School in Chicago in 1955, Pat had this idea that he could easily
make $100 a week in a factory. So he took an aptitude test and was
offered a job at Continental Can on the South Side. Starting pay
was $2.12 an hour. He thought he could do better, so he moved on

to Motorola, although his hourly pay was $1.66 an hour and he had to take three buses to get there. Fortunately, the main bosses were all Irish like himself, so he felt he had a better chance to advance there. It didn't happen, though, so he quit to work at a GM parts plant, starting at $2.50 an hour. Unfortunately, to move up in the GM pecking order, you literally had to wait for a worker to die, so after three months Pat was back at Motorola. He got engaged and at twenty-two married Laurie.

Despite a solid career that took him far in the company and six children to support, Pat said he had "had enough," so he quit in 1979 and bought some buildings and property to open a hot dog stand, which he later transformed into a restaurant and bar. He took all of his money out of his profit-sharing plan at Motorola to seed his real estate/restaurant business, which started out with five buildings. He also opened a sports bar and bought two apartment buildings.

Five years later, realizing that he had to put in 65 hours for every 40 hours of pay working for himself and that insurance premiums were eating up his profits, Pat sold most of the properties and rented out one building for a pizza place. With six kids he needed to make serious money and wondered how he would do it. Then Pat took the worst job of his life: manager-in-training at a floor-tile store. Although he was one of the top salespeople in his region, expenses charged back to him made it difficult to make decent money. It didn't help that Pat was also responsible for unloading trucks and scrubbing toilets at the store. Six months later he quit.

In 1983, Motorola was pioneering a radical new idea in telecommunications: the portable cellular phone. Although the early cell phones looked more like bulky, army-issue walkie-talkies, which Motorola made in World War II, the Schaumburg, Illinois–based company was ahead of the pack in design and manufacturing. When the cell phone wave first started, Motorola was the place to be, but it was humiliating for Pat to ask his former employer for his job back—they didn't return his calls for months. But Pat knew the company would once again reward his problem-solving and management skills and offer him a great opportunity. He was rehired in early 1984. His wife, Laurie, who had also worked there but had quit two years earlier, also returned.

Upon rejoining Motorola, Pat was re-vested in the company's pension plan and was offered a profit-sharing plan. All was going well again until fourteen years later, when the company announced a wave of cutbacks. Some fifteen thousand workers had to be laid off. By this time, though, Pat's children were all out of school and well on their own paths. He knew he could have retired at fifty-five, but "dollars still played a big part in my life." Although he wasn't in any danger of losing his job if he didn't take the early-retirement buyout the company offered him, his volunteer work called to him. After thirty-three years with the company, Pat and his wife decided to leave. He was fifty-seven. His exit package was generous: two years of salary, full pension, and health insurance that cost him $36 a month. The company even provided money for a financial planner and attorney.

Although he had become a passionate volunteer at a homeless shelter largely to find something to do while his kids were in school, Pat was avoiding the inevitable. He knew that one day he would have to look into the eyes of the homeless and see their misery. It was part of his rite of passage into a vocation of compassion, but not a rite he chose willingly. He worked in a homeless shelter largely at the suggestion of his pastor, Father Tom Enright, who was supervising Pat's parish commitment after Pat completed a program in pastoral studies. At first he chose the night shift, making sandwiches for the families that would leave the shelter in the morning, families Pat wouldn't see because he chose the 11 P.M. to 3 A.M. shift. He was an *organizer*, a man with a gift for detail and motivating others to get things done. Seeing despair wasn't something he was used to or could handle; there was nothing in his work life that had prepared him for it. Yet this is what he had been called to do. The road getting there had more curves in it than an Appalachian highway.

"I made damn sure I wouldn't be there when the bus pulled up to the homeless shelter," he recalled of his first experiences with Lake County PADS regional homeless shelter program. "I thought homeless shelters contained only men—bums. That was my idea when I volunteered as a site manager. I went there when they were sleeping so I really didn't have to see them. But then I *saw* them. There were *kids* in there. One mother had a three-month-old and was feeding the baby *chili*. There was no baby food available or a crib. I was fuming. My anger helped me over the situation. We got what we needed."

As you can see, Pat didn't waltz into his role as a pastoral volunteer overnight. However, in many ways his education in how to help people was just beginning. And his career path was hardly a straight, unbroken line. But it's clear that Pat has a passion for life that manifested itself the first day on the job and he's been nurturing it for fifty-eight years. In retirement, he's developing that passion in dozens of ways that most of us don't even consider when we're working.

Now Pat is one of the most enthusiastic and hardworking volunteers at Transfiguration Church, his home parish. In addition to helping run the homeless shelter and food pantry, he volunteers for the church's Parish Pastoral Council and St. Vincent DePaul Society, which assists families in need of food, clothing, and rent assistance. Working closely with elderly people, he trained to become a certified nurse's aide and takes patients back and forth from the hospital. Pat has also worked with Alzheimer's patients at the county nursing home. Trained in pastoral care, he's worked in hospitals, psychiatric wards, and hospices. Now he's going back to school to study bereavement counseling and has comforted many grieving families.

"There is a need [to help others]," he reflects. "The more I get involved and pray, the more I'm convinced I've gone and done the right thing."

If we are lucky, our passions and work overlap. But for many of us there is a boundary between our private passions and our work lives. Often our passionate interests don't consume us until we leave the office or factory floor. In some cases they may even haunt us in the workplace until we eventually acknowledge that conventional work has its place, but passionate pursuits are better. Pursuits that tug at our souls and engage our minds balance our lives by adding a spiritual dimension that may not come with a salary. In order to understand our passions, we need to dig deep into our personal ecology, especially if we haven't thought about it lately. While early retirement may give us the time to better divine those pursuits, we need to know that we can reward ourselves with that kind of life if we plan for it.

Assuming you've crunched the numbers and didn't get crunched yourself, you're ready for dessert. Now you can really slurp up the fun stuff. Do you have a passion? Would you like to pursue it? If your numbers look good—and you have your financial situation in control—now's the time to craft a passionate pursuit for yourself.

There's a long list of "passionate amateurs" who have changed society, the arts, or any field of endeavor they chose to pursue. Ben Franklin seeded the public library system and was a scientist, inventor, and statesman. Mother Jones led progressive political activism into the mainstream. Charles Ives was an insurance company executive who changed the course of Western classical music. Samuel Clemens left the Mississippi, headed west, and became Mark Twain. Each one of us has a Mark Twain or Mother Jones within us. We just need to know how to talk to them and draw them into the dialogue of our lives. You will have plenty of time in your early retirement, but you need tools to discover what your pursuits are and who you can be. Like Pat Gaughan, you may have had a solid idea all during your working life of what you wanted to do. Now's the time to fine-tune your plan.

Before we can identify and nurture the passionate amateurs within us, we need a better definition of work—one that doesn't split us in half as workers or nonworkers. This dichotomy must go in your new prosperity. E. F. Schumacher puts it sublimely when he writes in *Small Is Beautiful*: "To strive for leisure as an alternative to work would be considered a complete misunderstanding of one of the basic truths of human existence, namely that work and leisure are complementary parts of the same living process and can't be separated without destroying the joy of work and the bliss of leisure."

The Benefits of Passionate Pursuits

Myriad benefits can be derived from becoming an early retiree with a passionate pursuit. Among them are:

- A reengagement with life. Many of us are estranged from that which makes us feel most alive. You can rediscover your passions.

- A longer and healthier life. A recent MacArthur Foundation study, "Successful Aging," found that people who are engaged in life tended to have higher physical and cognitive functioning.

- You need to create a greater degree of *self-efficacy*, which improves physical and mental well-being, memory, and learning ability and results in an increased sense of personal competency later in life. According to the MacArthur study, "Older people high in self-efficacy are more likely to view memory as a set of cognitive skills that, to some extent at least, can be learned and improved."

- A greater satisfaction with life, spiritual enrichment, and something "you can leave behind." Your deeds are your legacy.

- An anti-stress outlet at any age. If you are actively engaged in a pursuit, it lasts the rest of your life. Doing something we love relaxes us.

- A cure for loneliness. If you are in need of meeting people, your passionate pursuit will get you connected fast. Courtesy of the Internet, you can find people like you all across the world, if not next door.

- An alternative to "time theft." Too many so-called activities steal our time and we feel more empty than entertained—commercials that litter every television show, sporting events and movies, "free" seminars that are really sales pitches for real estate or stockbrokers, etc. The time you spend with a passionate pursuit is entirely your own.

- A way to improve your neighborhood and society at large. If your neighborhood is falling apart, you are concerned about public education, or simply want to tackle the homeless problem, there are many ways of making completely personal contributions to society. You will be part of the solution.

- Remake your self. Aren't you tired of advertising that tells you how thin/beautiful/athletic/charming/smart you *should* be? Do something without buying any false cures. Invent a whole new persona based on what you *become*.

All we need to know is enclosed in the cocoon of our child-hoods. The actual shell of innocence may no longer embrace our harried lives, but the larval essence of what we need to know is still with us. We can still be passionate about things and transform them into our passionate pursuits. In many ways, it's essential that we do so if we're going to grow and thrive as individuals in a stress-filled information age. If we are to find fulfillment in a "retirement" that could last fifty years or more, we have to look at what makes us smile, challenges us in fresh and exciting ways, and propels us into an actively engaged future. Challenges, creativity, and the energy to do something lasting will sustain us better than any "youth serum" for the rest of our lives.

Redefining Work

Do you ever wonder what you'd do if you didn't have to work for money? Most of us have. Can you step into that picture that you create in your mind, given the financial scenario you've explored in earlier steps? The financial side of a new prosperity is actually the easier part intellectually, but now it's time to synthesize what you feel passionate about.

Doubtless you have plenty of sports, hobbies, and leisure activi-ties that keep you busy. But do they envelop your entire being or just provide a little stimulation? Now that you have the time to pursue anything you want, why not up the ante a bit? "We need to find activities that meet our needs separate from others, so that, when left alone, we can relish that sense of 'unholy aloneness' that will get us through the days when we feel lost and alone," suggests Dr. Barrie Sanford Greiff, a Harvard psychiatrist. As Carl Jung implores, "Turn the eye of consciousness within to see what is there. Let us see what we can do in small ways."

In order to end work as you know it, you need several new definitions of work and what passions drive the most meaningful parts of your life. If you think that all work is labor and drudgery, then let's explore some new ways of seeing labor. Work by itself is the employment of energy to do something. In the physical sense, you are expending electrochemical and mechanical energy, firing neurons and manifesting some electrochemical process.

So the idea of quitting *all* work is a myth that you probably need to put to rest. Suppose you have to take care of ailing parents or children? What if you get involved in community projects and you're called upon to use your talents and energy to build a church hall, a homeless shelter, or a symphony orchestra? It will require work, but the kind that merges with your soul's best intentions. Even if you have to change diapers (again), it could be called soul work because you are doing it with and for someone you love. I'm not trying to give nasty work a good name—that could be called "negative labor." The key here is to realize that work in its many forms should be supported by a flexible new prosperity plan.

Whatever work you undertake should be closer to William Morris's "work-pleasure," where any kind of work is done for the personal satisfaction of doing something well. Morris found pleasure in working with his hands in creating beautiful printing, wallpaper patterns, stained-glass windows, and paintings. He merged work and passion in a century that institutionalized hatred for manual labor.

William Morris accomplished so much in his lifetime apart from his successful design business that when he passed away one of his elegies paid him the ultimate compliment: "He died of being William Morris." Living at the height of the first Industrial Revolution, Morris believed that industrialization would free workers to pursue a life filled with art and beauty. Like Franklin, he had a vision of a nonwork life that didn't involve the equivalent of watching videos, drinking beer, or perusing shopping malls. Along with the critic and writer John Ruskin, Morris stressed handcrafting, worker freedom, creativity, and organic design. His heirs included

Louis Sullivan and Frank Lloyd Wright. Their ideas influenced everything from the Prairie style in architecture to Mission furniture and are very much with us today as we seek alternatives to the information age.

Envisioning a world in which workers would be freed by labor-saving devices to enjoy the world more, Morris noted toward the end of his life about leisure time: "I should often do some direct good to the community with it, by practicing arts or occupations for my hands or brain which would give pleasure to many of the citizens; in other words, a great deal of the best work done would be done in the leisure time of men relieved from any anxiety as to their livelihood, and eager to exercise their special talent."

What *you* call work depends on the context. All work consumes energy, but there are subtle differences. The following table gives open-ended definitions of different kinds of work. These definitions are mere guidelines for reinterpreting work and merging it with your own passions. Fill in your own types of work and see if your perspective on labor may be seen in a different light.

TYPES OF WORK: NEW PROSPERITY DEFINITIONS

Type	Requires	Examples
Labor/Pure-Work	Physical/Light Mental	Digging holes, washing dishes, changing diapers
Passion-Work	Physical/Mental/ Spiritual	Labor that satisfies whole being, life projects
Soul-Work	Physical/Mental/ Spiritual	Community/ religious volunteer work, arts
Love-Work	Mental/Physical/ Spiritual	Child-raising, caregiving

Type	Requires	Examples
Leisure-Work	Mostly Mental/ Light Physical	Hobbies, crafts, gardening
Body-Work	Mostly Physical/ Light Mental	Exercise, sports, walking
Livelihood-Work	Varying degrees of each	That which you primarily do for income

Your Own Work Types (Fill in the blanks)

Type	Describe Activity Involved
Passion-Work	_____
Soul-Work	_____
Love-Work	_____
Leisure-Work	_____
Body-Work	_____
Livelihood-Work	_____

You may notice some overlap and apparent contradictions. How can leisure activities be considered work? Can't you be passionate about washing dishes? Are exercise and volunteerism work? Don't you do these things away from work? All of these activities involve some expenditure of effort and physical, mental, or spiritual involvement. They are not passive activities, therefore they fit into combined definitions of what work is. In this context, there is no such thing as a negative activity—so these types of work can be rewarding on many different levels.

Can you find spiritual comfort while digging a hole? Sure. The mind-body union (if you want to be Zen about it) can be an enriching experience. You're communing with the earth. Can you truly be working while painting a picture or playing golf?

Absolutely. All of these activities burn calories, employ physical faculties, and require that you expend some effort to do them. How you see these different types of work will help you distill your passions. Let's say you have a passion for caregiving. You may want to volunteer in a nursing home (or become a nurse's aide). God knows they can use your help. Or you have a passion for being with kids. The local school district could use your talents. Dick Parker in step 2 was active helping kids in school. In other words, match your passion to the type of work you want to do—and that may need to be done in your community.

What Are Your Passionate Pursuits?

Are you prepared for the new kinds of work that may enhance your life? Over the last century, we've been consumed by the Protestant work ethic, the rise of professionalism, and a society where a successful career is paramount in climbing the social ladder. If you're truly seeking a new prosperity, then different forms of work I've detailed can be performed passionately. This time, however, you won't be doing the work for money.

My extended definition of passionate pursuits, however, goes beyond having a devotion to dancing, scuba diving, or sewing. It's an activity that offers you the potential of a total revelation and transformation of self that extends our souls into our family, community, and society. A pursuit isn't a pastime, like watching baseball games or soap operas, which may involve us on a superficial and passive level. I'm referring to a deeper commitment, an activity that involves all of our being. This pursuit engages our personal ecology and may lead us to what Thomas Moore calls "soul work," or that joyful, spirit-enhancing set of activities that makes us feel most alive and that we would gladly do without pay. I'm not addressing activities such as television watching, sports events, boating, hunting, fishing, or any number of hobbies or crafts.

Using my definition of passionate pursuits, take a moment and reflect upon your passions and how they can enhance your new prosperity. What were you doing in the past during your working career and what would you like to do now? It's possible you've lost interest in some things and renewed your interest in others. Jot a few ideas down and review them in a week or so. Then figure out which ones you can pursue and how you would go about pursuing them.

YOUR PASSIONATE PURSUITS: A BRIEF INVENTORY

During Working Career	Would Like to Pursue Now
1.	1.
2.	2.
3.	3.
4.	4.
5.	5.

Your Passions Can Change the World

It's important to realize that what drives our passion is something we need in order to direct our life beyond retirement. It's fuel for our daily pursuits. But passion without focus is like a camera without a lens. You need to studiously develop your interests, but have fun in the process. You will be working for the love of doing something, so there's no pressure to perform, only discover.

NEW PROSPERITY TIP

One of the best ways of rediscovering our passions is to open up our high school yearbooks and see what we were involved in. Which of these activities do you want to build upon now?

Benjamin Franklin was as much a passionate amateur as he was an inventor, scientist, statesman, printer, and any of a dozen other "labels." After starting a successful printing business and publishing *Poor Richard's Almanac* for twenty-five years, he was able to live a life of his own choosing at a fairly young age. The *Almanac* alone made him wealthy and famous on both sides of the Atlantic, but despite his fortune, Franklin embarked upon a life of discovery and public service.

Unlike Washington and Jefferson, Franklin never retreated to the life of a country gentleman on a huge estate manned by slaves but chose to experiment with electricity, found a college, start a library, and do even more commonplace things like pave the streets of Philadelphia and ensure they were cleaned every day. Franklin's public life is well documented as are his many inventions and scientific observations, such as charting the Gulf Stream. What is more intriguing about Franklin is why he chose the life he did, which arguably he would have pursued had he not been financially secure.

Franklin had a compelling concept of what he should do with his leisure time, which in his case occupied the rest of his long life, from the age of forty-two to eighty-four. Unlike our modern, postindustrial idea of buying a place somewhere in the Sun Belt and golfing a lot, Franklin chose to work at what Marsha Sinetar, author of *Do What You Love, The Money Will Follow,* calls the "creative passion or challenge" of his life. In his age, as in ours, many social problems beckoned him. So he responded in personal fashion.

When Franklin invented his famous stove, which was a quantum leap in home heating of the time, he chose not to patent it. He originally called it the "Pennsylvania" stove and made its plans available through a free pamphlet. Unlike inefficient fireplaces that sucked most of the heat out of a room, the Franklin stove radiated a large percentage of heat back *into* a room. That was a big advance in heating for the eighteenth century and made for much more comfortable rooms and saved on wood consumption. Despite the fact that he knew that others would make a fortune from his design, he remarked that "as we enjoy great advantages from the inventions of others, we should be glad of an opportunity to serve others by any invention of ours; and this we should do freely and generously."

Franklin also injected a sense of moral and social responsibility into his non-career pursuits that is sorely missing from our stock-market-obsessed time. As he elaborates in his still-relevant *Poor Richard's Almanac,* "Leisure is time for doing something useful."

Because of his hundreds of other activities, Franklin never finished his masterpiece on the *Art of Virtue,* which he began as a young man. Nevertheless, he took to heart Cicero's advice that "leisure consists in all those virtuous activities by which a man grows morally, intellectually, and spiritually. It is that which makes a life worth living."

Until this century, passionate pursuits would drive a number of geniuses who nurtured their gifts and contributed immeasurably to society and culture. Here's a short list of famous people who made a living at one thing, but became known for their passionate pursuits:

PASSIONATE AMATEURS IN HISTORY

Person	Original Occupation	Passionate Pursuit
Aesop	Advocate (lawyer)	Writer
Marcus Aurelius	Roman emperor	Poet, philosopher
Leonardo DaVinci	Artist	Scientist, inventor
Thomas More	Politician	Philosopher, writer
Charles Darwin	Gentleman	Naturalist
Richard F. Burton	Translator	Explorer, writer
William Morris	Designer	Writer, painter, translator
Leo Tolstoy	Landowner	Novelist
Anton Chekhov	Doctor	Playwright
Samuel Clemens	Riverboat pilot	Author
Charles Ives	Insurance executive	Composer

Person	Original Occupation	Passionate Pursuit
William Carlos Williams	Doctor	Poet
Edgar Lee Masters	Lawyer	Poet
Albert Einstein	Patent clerk	Scientist

This list could go on with countless famous persons who ended up pursuing their passion after succeeding (and sometimes failing) at other things. One of the most famous amateurs, Thomas Edison, was an ace telegraph operator and never took a single class in engineering. All of his pursuits began as amateur interests. He was curious and brilliant and wanted to improve the world. His tinkerings led to what we now know as the Second Industrial Revolution. Sometimes the motivation to improve society is the most essential factor in motivating passionate amateurs. That yearning for something better often leads to powerful social movements.

Unfortunately, the aforementioned list is dominated largely by dead, white European and American males. With a few exceptions, due to a male-dominated society, women had few options outside of marriage and motherhood. There are, of course, great artists such as Hildegard of Bingen, George Sand, Mary Cassatt, and Georgia O'Keeffe, although they found their passions at an early age. No matter who you are, you'll need to identify your calling by first seeing within yourself and pulling out your passions and putting them on the kitchen table for closer examination. With the financial security that comes with a new prosperity and early retirement, there will be little or no pressure for you to turn these passions into businesses or forms of income. Just relax and enjoy yourself.

How do we embrace life with the infinite romance that we are told exists only in utopias? The first step is to acknowledge our inner needs, that our life could be fuller, that we need to express another part of us in order to be whole.

We need to ask some basic questions, which this book will guide you through (more on this in steps 9 and 10). In short, we need to admit what Saul Bellow calls "an immense, painful longing for a broader, more flexible, fuller, more coherent, more comprehensive account of what we human beings are, who we are, and what this life is for."

Finding and Building on Your Passion

1. Know the different kinds of work and see how they relate to your life.

2. Choose a passionate pursuit or two and invest yourself in them.

3. Follow that pursuit by educating yourself and sharing it with others.

4. Keep yourself on track by practicing that passion and letting it enrich and inform you.

Fully Funding the Vehicles to Get You Out Early

In the long run, it's not just how much money you make that will determine your future prosperity. It's how much of that money you put to work by saving and investing it.

—Peter Lynch

At first glance, Marsha McBroom was intimidated. Boeing's Renton, Washington, plant was gargantuan and made large jets with millions of parts. Skeletons of 757s were in various stages of assembly. It was a construction site of aluminum and steel, only the skeletons were not becoming buildings but mammoth metal birds. Men were crawling over them like ants, installing wires, hydraulic systems, rudders, wings. Marsha was thirty-four when she walked into the plant as the only woman on her crew in 1979.

"When I first started, the men sent me into the tool room to get a 'wire stretcher,' so I went. There was no such thing. I was constantly being razzed. I was there because it paid two dollars more an hour than working as a clerk at Nordstrom's warehouse. I had just a high school education and was a homemaker. I was hired with no knowledge."

Despite her rough start, Boeing provided all the on-the-job training Marsha needed and she thrived. Management also became more enlightened. Instead of yelling at workers to get things done, over time there were discussions about work duties. Hired as a mechanic, Marsha learned fast and moved into management six years later. Eventually becoming a first-line manager, she had twenty to forty mechanics working for her installing wiring. When she first started work, the managers were constantly screaming and yelling at workers. After a few years that changed, too, and she fell into the work and enjoyed being a manager, "always feeling like I belonged."

Working on the Boeing 757 since its inception, Marsha went home from work with a sense of accomplishment; she was comforted by the fact that she could talk to upper management in the early years. While the company invested in her, Marsha also invested in herself through the company's 401(k) plan, sticking with stock index funds for growth. Although Boeing offered a generous matching contribution to her 401(k), 50% matching on the first 8% contributed, she contributed only the minimum for years, a move she corrected in later years when she boosted her contribution to 15% and the company boosted their matching contribution to 75% on the first 8% contributed by Marsha.

Her husband, a computer consultant, wasn't saving as much as she was, although he owned an IRA but no other pension plans. Nevertheless, they lived comfortably in suburban Seattle, owned a motor home, and consolidated its payments with their mortgage by refinancing. They also owned some property. Their life was going fairly well.

Marsha enjoyed managing the building of 737 aircraft, the most popular commercial jet in the sky, yet regretted that she didn't have enough time to visit her two sons, who were in their thirties, and her grandchildren. So when Boeing announced a series of voluntary layoffs in October 1998, she gave a close look to what the company was offering. The money looked enticing: one week of pay for every year served. With twenty years behind her, that was a healthy package to start. She was also fully vested in the company's pension plan and had $268,000 in her 401(k). The company would pay her health insurance premiums in full until she reached sixty-two in the early-retirement plan. But Marsha still needed time to run the numbers and see if it was worth her while to take the money and quit.

Doing some math, Marsha calculated that if she stayed, she'd be making the equivalent of a $2.75-an-hour differential less between taking the lump sum and staying on at her salary level. Since her husband said he was going to continue working for at least another four years, the decision became easier. In January of 1999 at the age of fifty-four, she said good-bye to Boeing, her salary of $68,850, and became one of the first of her co-workers to take the buyout.

"As one of the first ones to do it [take early retirement], I became the expert on the subject. People came to me and called all the time asking about it. I was happy with the departure and comfortable."

Now Marsha has the time she needs not only for her grandkids, but for her sons, parents, and husband. She stopped employing landscapers to do her yard and was even gratified to have the time to clean the house for her daughter-in-law. When her husband retires, they're off in their motor home for a long trip to western states.

Now that she has "time left at the end of the day," Marsha is glad that she took time to learn about mutual funds and retirement planning early in her career. Here's a key part of what she learned:

- She used stock-index funds as the mainstay of her 401(k). Although she didn't invest the maximum amount at first in the funds, she later moved to fully fund them.

- When she retired, she rolled over her 401(k) assets into a family of mutual funds and opened a low-cost brokerage account (.08% a year). She doesn't plan to withdraw any of the 401(k) funds until her husband retires and then plans to take out only 3% per year and keep the remainder growing (in stock funds).

- She performed monthly payment projections and figured she wouldn't need more money until she's ninety-four (that's as far as her projections go). A regular user of the Internet, she's scanned the major mutual fund sites, all of which feature free retirement planning information.

- Of the funds she invests in, 75% of her money is in eleven S&P stock index funds and 25% in four bond mutual funds. She can make transactions through an automated phone system and the Internet, but doesn't move her money around.

- After learning that she could probably average 10% a year in returns, she had most of her money in the stock-index fund while employed. "I didn't mind the risk," she said.

- Although she tried out the services of three financial planners, upon further education she found out they tacked on management fees that ate into her returns, so she decided she was the best person to manage her retirement funds and took full control of them herself.

Your Core Prosperity Plan Portfolio Funds

The truth is, as Marsha McBroom demonstrated, that to beat inflation and earn decent returns for your new prosperity portfolio you have to do very little in terms of managing your money. Marsha has a majority of her retirement funds in stock-index mutual funds, which invest in broad-based indexes of stocks. That means you don't have to worry if your hot stock pick will perform next year or when to sell it. You don't have to track down last year's blistering mutual funds and then pull your money out when they come up short the following year. You don't even have to take the bad advice of a broker, who has no interest in whether your investment performs at all—brokers make money on commissions, not performance.

If you invest in a core of mutual funds that do all of the heavy lifting for you, you can enjoy far more of your retirement than you thought possible. Some 77 million Americans invested more than $5 trillion in mutual funds (according to the Investment Company Institute) for an excellent reason: somebody else is doing most of the work for you. It comes down to two basic concepts that will beat most managed mutual funds and stocks for the next several decades: the low costs and returns of index funds often beat the majority of stock mutual funds. I know this is hardly glamorous, but this strategy is consistent and easy. Leave your money alone for decades. You won't have to time the market, find a hot manager, pull out during a downturn or get burned when a (non-indexing) manager thinks there's downturn and keeps you out of the market—during a rally. Not only are you probably going to beat the lion's share of managers out there, *your total return will be higher because the expenses of running the fund may be up to three times lower.*

Nobody beats the market consistently. Even the hottest fund managers slink back to the market average eventually, which statisticians call "regression to the mean (average)." What is the market *average?* It's a benchmark based on an index of stocks. The most commonly used index is the Standard & Poor's 500, which is a basket of the five hundred largest industrial corporations. Although the S&P has done handsomely over the past decade, it's but a tenth of the total stock market, which includes mid-cap, small-cap, or international stocks. "Cap" is short for capitalization, or the value of a stock based on its stock price times the number of outstanding shares. It used to be that only "blue chips" like IBM, GM, and Exxon were large caps, but the frenzy in technology and Internet stocks has pushed a lot of small companies (many without any earnings) into large- or mid-cap status.

The beauty of an index—or a mutual fund that invests in the index, called a *stock-index fund*—is manifold. Through an index, you get consistent diversification. An S&P 500 index invests in the same 500 stocks all the time. A Wilshire 5000 fund invests in nearly all listed U.S. stocks. Because these funds are considered "unmanaged"—that is, there's no buying or selling of stocks, they're held all the time—there are no brokerage commissions to reduce your total return. These funds are also relatively *tax efficient,* meaning they don't trigger much, if any, capital gains, which you have to pay taxes on outside of a tax-deferred account. The most splendid thing about these funds is that they are robustly diversified and beat most managed funds most of the time. So you don't have to pick last year's hot fund manager who may have a portfolio loaded with out-of-favor stocks this year. The funds listed below also sport low management expenses, no sales charges, and the flexibility of going with a large fund company, which provides dozens of support services.

S & P 500 INDEX VS. EQUITY MUTUAL FUNDS (ANNUAL RETURNS FOR PERIODS ENDED DECEMBER 31, 1997)

Period (Years)	S&P 500 Index	Average Equity Mutual Fund	Index Advantage
50	13.1%	11.8%	1.3%
40	12.3	11.5	0.8
30	12.5	10.8	1.7
25	14.3	13.9	0.4
20	17.4	15.6	1.8
15	17.2	13.2	4.0
10	18.6	15.2	3.4
5	23.1	18.1	5.0

Source: The Vanguard Group

You may argue that index funds take a lot of the adventure out of stock investing. Well, index funds are kind of *boring,* although profitable. If you need a little excitement in your prosperity portfolio, either choose individual stocks (read on) or spice up your portfolio with higher-risk (and more volatile) "high-flyer funds," such as those listed below:

SUGGESTED PROSPERITY PORTFOLIOS

Fund	Allocation of Total Prosperity Portfolio	Phone (800)	Web site (http://www.)
Vanguard Index 500 or Vanguard Total Market Index	50%	662-7447	vanguard.com
Schwab 1000	20%	435-4000	schwab.com
Vanguard Small-Cap Index	20%	662-7447	vanguard.com
Vanguard Total International	10%	662-7447	vanguard.com

HIGH-FLYER FUNDS
(REPLACE TWO FUNDS ABOVE
IF YOU CAN ACCEPT MORE MARKET RISK)

Fund			
Vanguard Health Care	15–25%	662-7447	vanguard.com
T. Rowe Price Science & Technology	15%	638-5660	troweprice.com
Third Avenue Value	10%	443-1021	n/a
Baron Asset	10%	992-2766	n/a

These funds were selected for the combination of low cost and high performance. Similar index funds may be offered in your 401(k) plan. If so, then employ the suggested allocations. You can adjust the allocations to suit market conditions. The S&P 500, which has been the best-performing index through 1998, probably won't continue its hot streak, so you can reallocate your money to the more promising index. Keep in mind there's some overlap between the S&P 500 index, Schwab 1000, and the Wilshire or "Total Market" index. For most investors, the Wilshire will cover most listed U.S. stocks. The small-cap and international indexes give you some more market coverage and can be boosted when those markets perk up. Keep in mind that although the S&P 500 index has beat most stock mutual funds in twelve out of the last fifteen years, that's not a permanent trend. Small-caps and international stocks run in hot cycles as well, so it pays to buy index funds to fully diversify your portfolio.

NEW PROSPERITY TIP

Fund fees can really gnaw away at your total returns over time. A 1% annual fund fee will reduce your final account balance by 18% on an investment held for twenty years. Ask every fund manager for the "expense ratio" on their funds, which is the annual amount deducted for fees, administration, and brokerage commissions. *Never buy a fund with any kind of "load " or sales charge, 12(b) 1 fee, or "contingent deferred sales charge."* While this advice is a golden rule in boosting your fund returns, only 8% of fund investors surveyed understood the fees charged by their funds, according to the Securities and Exchange Commission. Know how much in fees are being charged and find fund managers with the lowest fees and the highest-available returns.

Getting Vigilant About Your Company Retirement Plan

So you've fully funded your own plans and are comfortable with your company plan. Is it time to sit back, relax, and let the miracle of tax-free compounding do its magic? Your work is not over quite yet. There's more to be done. Here are some items to bird-dog that will help you maximize your investment.

■ **What is the fee structure of your plan?** Typically, the plan administrator takes a certain percentage—or flat fee—of funds under management. The flat-fee arrangement is usually the better deal. The fund managers will take a percentage of your funds every year to manage the money. Although you probably have no control over the fee structure (unless you choose the manager yourself), you can find out how much these fees are eating into your returns. Since there are thousands of companies competing to manage and administer 401(k) and similar plans, you can request that your employer shop around for lower fees if you feel you're being gouged. For example, my company plan offered an index fund, but it was underperforming the index by a full 1.5 percentage points, which is deplorable considering there's hardly any management involved in an index fund. I agitated within my company to bring some other funds into the 401(k) plan—and eventually they did.

- **Do you have enough funds in your plan?** Generally, you need only a handful of funds to diversify properly. Beyond a certain point, the number of funds you invest in can get in the way of your efforts to pick the right combination of risk for your prosperity portfolio. At the core of your holdings—at least 60 percent of your total portfolio—should be stocks (within index funds). Small-cap, international, value, and mid-cap funds are also important to your mix. Several types of income funds give you a choice between government, corporate, and mortgage bonds, but they're not too useful in a tax-deferred fund since you are primarily interested in building growth. Then there are several hybrid funds that straddle the mix between growth and income, such as balanced (stocks and bonds), equity-income (high-dividend stocks), and combinations of every kind of fund type. While you can always lower your risk with these latter kinds of funds, your total return will drop as well. Remember, 92 percent of your investment success will depend on the mix of funds you pick. You won't be successful if your money is spread among twenty funds or you're not zeroing in on stock funds for growth.

- **The ability to switch between funds may be overrated (and abused).** Some 401(k)s have gotten so advanced that you can switch between funds using a 24-hour automated phone service or through the Internet. While this is a technological advance, if overused it may hamper your ability to make money consistently. In fact, constant monitoring and switching of funds is a really bad idea. More often than not, you'll be spooked by a market downturn, then pull out when the market's down and move back in when the market's high. This is the exact opposite of what you should be doing. Another habit you'll want to avoid is being able to see your account balances on a daily or even hourly basis move up and down with the market ebbs and flows. It's fine to check balances now and again, but save your allocation and switching decisions for the end of the year. If there are funds that are under-performing—unless the market as a whole had a down year—then make the appropriate moves.

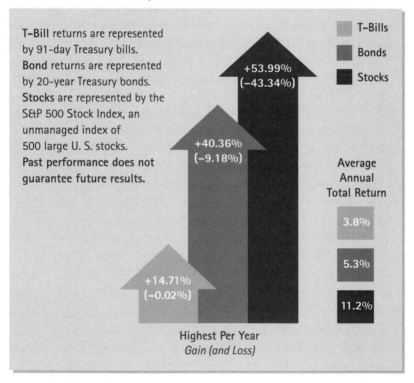

LONG-TERM INVESTMENT RESULTS: BEST (AND WORST) YEARS
January 1, 1926–December 31, 1998

T–Bill returns are represented by 91-day Treasury bills.
Bond returns are represented by 20-year Treasury bonds.
Stocks are represented by the S&P 500 Stock Index, an unmanaged index of 500 large U. S. stocks.
Past performance does not guarantee future results.

T–Bills
Bonds
Stocks

+53.99%
(−43.34%)

+40.36%
(−9.18%)

Average Annual Total Return

3.8%

5.3%

+14.71%
(−0.02%)

11.2%

Highest Per Year
Gain (and Loss)

Source: The Hartford

- **What do I do with new money?** It's incredibly tempting to take your raise in cash and not save it. Unfortunately, you have to pay taxes if it makes its way into your paycheck. You do much better if you invest it in your plan using pretax dollars (only FICA is withheld). You're saving more and paying less in taxes.

Buying Individual Stocks for Growth

Despite what they say on *Wall Street Week*, CNBC, and in any financial publication you can name, there is no magic strategy to picking stocks that grow over time. Yet, there's certainly a lot of predictability in buying stock in a well-managed company that's growing. Of course, industries, markets, products, and even management change over time. But as an institution it's in the best interest of a company to keep making money over time.

How do you find consistently profitable companies? A handful of guidelines are generally accepted among growth-stock investors. These criteria combine what you need in a stock in order for your overall portfolio to be successful over the next few decades:

1. **Pick a company that has earnings growth of at least 15% per year. That means the stock price will double in about five years.** This is not a hard and fast figure, since you can probably get away with something growing at 12% or better. The key is consistency. You can find these stocks quite easily by reading the *Wall Street Journal, Barron's, Investors Business Daily,* or by going to the library and perusing *Value Line Investment Survey* or *Standard & Poor's.*

2. **The company should have quality management that boosts sales, creates new products or services, and is boosting market share every year.** Consistent management and innovation are the key to growth in a quality company. If a company is not increasing sales, then you won't see any corresponding increase in the stock price.

3. **Diversify your portfolio among industries and countries.** Some multinational companies, like GE, Procter & Gamble, Colgate-Palmolive, and others already sell a huge product line across the globe. Make sure not to load up on stocks in any one industry. That will raise your overall portfolio risk. A dozen stocks in technology, pharmaceuticals, consumer products, utilities, manufacturing, financial services, food, health care, telecommunications, and other businesses should round out your prosperity portfolio. You want companies that are still making money in thirty years. If you do your homework right the first time—just hang on to the stock and keep reinvesting in it—your "buy and hold" approach will pay dividends.

4. **Invest and reinvest for total return.** Total return is a combination of low transaction costs, share-price appreciation, dividend payouts, and reinvestment. The most efficient way of maximizing total return is through dividend-reinvestment (DRIP) or direct-purchase plans (DPP). With DRIPs and DPPs, you are taking one share and putting it into a special account that will automatically reinvest quarterly dividends and allow you to purchase new shares without paying a brokerage commission. When shares split, you can also buy more shares at lower prices. The best way to work DRIPs is to purchase one share through a discount broker, then tell the broker to deposit the share in a DRIP plan (you'll have to call the company's investor relations department and fill out the paperwork). Then you can bypass the broker and buy shares at no cost. You'll get a statement every quarter and can sell at any time at a nominal fee. The DPP is the same setup, only you don't even need to use a broker for the first share—you buy it directly from the company, which also sets up your DRIP. When you've selected some stocks, call the company to see if they have a DRIP or DPP.

5. **Monitor your companies, but don't sell unless something devastating happens to the corporation.** All of your companies will have ups and downs. That's the nature of the market. Technology companies will get battered at the end of a product cycle. Phar-

maceuticals get burned whenever there's talk in Congress of national health care. Every industry has its Achilles' heel. That's why you diversify and see if anything catastrophic is going on with your companies. Read the newspaper. Check the Internet (see Resources at the end of the book for the best financial Web sites). Often downturns are perfect opportunities to buy more shares through your DRIP plans.

Join an Investment Club to Learn and Earn

The best way to learn about stock picking is to join or form an investment club. Anyone can join and learn in a social setting. Two books ago, when my wife, Kathleen, was reading over my manuscript for *The Investment Club Book* (Warner, 1995), she decided that our family needed to start one. So she recruited me, my two brothers-in-law, two sisters-in-law, her mom and dad, and one friend. Although two sisters-in-law and one brother-in-law dropped out (one due to a divorce), the club is thriving and is getting better every month by learning the subtle details of finding a long-term performer.

The single best resource for investment clubbers is the nonprofit National Association of Investors Corporation (877-275-6242 or www.better-investing.org). Not only will they provide the materials for starting up a club, they publish an excellent magazine called *Better Investing* (you get it when you join) that is written for any level of investor. The publication also lists DRIPs and stock suggestions and walks you through the fundamental analysis of stocks.

A Sample Stock Portfolio

How many individual stocks you own is a function of how much time you have to research and monitor them. If you can research and manage a dozen stocks, that's a good start, provided they give you diversification across industries. If you own an index fund in addition to your individual issues, this is a moot point, however. Individual stocks should only be bought if you do the homework or through an investment-club setting. You will need to learn the fundamentals of stock picking. A portfolio is like a garden, it needs constant attention in the form of pruning, weeding, and fertilization.

There is no reliable rule on how many stocks you should own, although it's suggested that the more stocks you have representing major industries, the lower your overall risk profile. You can own stocks in addition to mutual funds, inside of a brokerage-house IRA or in a non-tax-deferred account. No matter what you do, keep in mind that a stock is like a horse and needs constant feeding, grooming, and attention. The following is a sample portfolio of "The Wall Street Prowlers," my family's investment club. It's by no means the one you should assemble, but we're proud to say it has produced an (unaudited) compound annual return of 38.17% since December 31, 1997.

A SAMPLE PORTFOLIO: THE WALL STREET PROWLERS' PICKS

Stock	Industry	Notes
Merck	Pharmaceuticals	Admired management and products, growth
Motorola	Phones, radios, etc.	Constant innovation in telecommunications
Oracle	Database software	Steady growth, little competition, great product
RPM	Coatings	Numerous splits, recession-proof
Sysco	Food service	Recession-proof, well managed
Walgreen's	Retail drug chain	Keeps expanding, stock splits

Now That You Have Your Vehicles, Let's Hit the Road!

1. Choose stock-index funds for consistent returns, low management expenses, and diversification. Buy them and keep them as the core of your prosperity portfolio.

2. If you have the time to research and monitor individual stocks, select them for consistent annual earnings growth of 15%, solid management, and innovation. Diversify across industries.

3. Invest in stocks that have DRIPs and DPPs to reduce costs and buy more shares on a consistent basis.

4. If you are just starting out—or want to turn stock investing into a fun social event—then join an investment club.

How to Retire Early Even If You Have Kids at Home

Whoever perpetrated the mathematical inaccuracy "Two can live as cheaply as one" has a lot to answer for.

—Caren Meyer

You know immediately from entering Al and Laura Mussman's stunning home that they are fully engaged with the passionate muses of creativity and vitality. Sculptures, fountains, and paintings adorn the white contemporary house. From the front deck on the third floor, you can see the skyscrapers of downtown Chicago looming across Lake Michigan. They are a few feet from a beach in this enclave of the rare and splendid Indiana Dunes. This is the place they want to be and seem to glow every time they walk out on the deck, which is as laid-back as a California beach house. They're nestled between a major metropolis, steel mills, power plants, and a natural preserve where herons roost while trucks roar by.

The Mussmans exude a joy that comes only with being at peace with what they're doing and being able to share it—with their sons Reece, ten, and Clark, eight. Not only is it an adult paradise, the soccer field and basketball court are just down the street. Their church, police station, and village hall are all within walking distance of their home, which has a post that greets you in Spanish, Swahili, Italian, and English.

Out of Indiana University and married in 1979 to Laura, Al studied voice and opera at Indiana's renowned school of music. When his favorite voice teacher died, his music career seemed less enticing to him and he accepted his father's offer to join the family business as a subfranchisor of Dairy Queen restaurants in northwestern Indiana. By 1982, Al and Laura had their own store and worked it so well that they tripled sales and ranked among the top ten Dairy Queens in the nation in product volume. Laura worked alongside Al but hated the business, so she went to school to study interior design. After seven years in a restaurant and five years in a territory office, Al and Laura were able to buy out his father's interest, although Al still wasn't quite sure he wanted to do it.

Then a break came. In 1995, the parent company (International Dairy Queen) offered to buy the Mussmans out by offering a deferred payment and regular income. He took the offer. He was only forty at the time. Although the sale allowed him to breath easier and devote as much time as he wanted to his sons, Laura discovered she had a malignant tumor in her breast. Although they would net a windfall from the sale in a few years, it paled in comparison to the fight Laura went through with chemotherapy. Al spent time with Laura and occupied his spare time helping out at his church.

Freed from the business, he expended his energies in helping a Vietnam vet, volunteering at church, and building homes for Habitat for Humanity in Mexico and Mississippi. In a heartbeat, he jokingly admits he became "the Church Lady." As a marathon runner, he has the physique and mien of an athlete who lives to consume endorphins. But like a runner starting to fatigue, he felt he was *too* involved with his volunteer activities. The rush was gone.

"I wasn't comfortable with being so involved, it felt like I was wearing a mask. Volunteering started to feel like work, so I said to my friend the pastor I had to stop, and I retired as church deacon."

One of the greatest benefits of being at home for Al is that he's with his sons any time they need him. He's there to drive them to soccer practice, which is just down the street. If they want to play basketball, they can shoot hoops a few blocks away. If they want to play on the beach, it's across the street. He and Laura retired to their dream house on the lake because it's the idyllic life they wanted, where they wanted to live it.

Of course, they are saving modestly for college educations, but when the Dairy Queen deal starts paying off in full in 2005 (they structured a delayed payment), there will be abundant cash to invest and all of their financial needs will be more than satisfied. They negotiated a lease-buyout option that will create a windfall in five years. Until then, they have an income stream from their properties to support them.

Soon after he took a break from his volunteer work, however, Laura's cancer relapsed, this time with a vengeance resulting in brain tumors and other maladies. Despite the two U-turns in their lives, Al remains optimistic to the point of planning to launch a new business and is grateful he can be there for Laura and his sons.

"I'm available for Laura. I know lots of families where two people *have* to work. I don't have to juggle anything else. I'm able to be interrupted at any time."

Undaunted, Al is not only starting a business designing water gardens but he's refurbishing an investment property he bought in his neighborhood. The splendid water garden he built that I saw gurgled contentedly in a neighbor's backyard cradled by boulders and a picturesque waterfall. By honoring his commitments beyond work, Al has developed some invaluable insights into how to balance his needs with his family life:

- He structured his business sale so that he would have a modest income stream for a few years, then a large payout. In the meantime, he's set up automatic withdrawals from the income stream into mutual funds to fuel long-term savings for his family.

- Although he's a runner by nature and practice, Al's discovered that "it's okay to be lazy and spend all day writing letters and hanging out."

- He's come to the realization that few things can really be resolved in a relationship, but if he's just there, that's enough. "It's about love, we just see a small part of the picture in our skin."

- Even though he retired at a relatively young age, he still regards himself as a rugged individualist who needs to experiment to see how life works. He has no training or background in building water gardens, yet knows he can succeed by teaching himself what he needs to know. He's also working with an architect and team of contractors in refurbishing his investment property.

- In demonstrating that a sound personal ecology is always being tested, he concentrates on relationships and not the pain of living. "The big picture is love and relationships. You have to keep that in focus. Can you bring love to a situation? Can you accept love? When you receive love, you are giving a gift to somebody else. We're missing the boat if we don't see that."

You Can Have a New Prosperity While the Kids Are at Home

Cradling your child in your arms makes you realize how little everything else is worth because you know, at that instant, your child is the light through which humanity itself is illuminated. One of the sublime pleasures of being a thoughtful parent is not only that you're preparing your children for the world in your own way, but if you've done your job right, you're helping the world become a better place. Parenting as altruism—what a concept! So how you prepare your children for the world will allow them to develop their own well-balanced personal ecology.

You're probably wondering, though, how in the heck am I ever going to retire if I'm staring down six-figure college bills, a mortgage, a car payment, and all the attendant bills of daily living? Well, that's just the situation I'm in as I write this book, but my new prosperity plan includes both college savings and retirement funding. You can do both by fully funding your company plans—in my case my 401(k) and SEP-IRAs—an Education IRA and a Roth IRA. In case you didn't read step 6, go back and check out the details. Since I'll be fifty-nine when my daughter starts college, that money will be available tax-free for her education.

Not everyone is in the same situation I am. My daughter Sarah Virginia graced this world when I turned forty (I married my Belfast beauty Kathleen Rose when I turned thirty after a robust bachelorhood as a Chicago-based journalist). I have company. I've met dads in their fifties. I know one company president who's in his sixties and has toddlers. So I'm not exactly the worst example in the world. If you get a late start in marriage or enter into a second or third marriage to a younger spouse, a lot of things are possible given the advances in fertility science.

So, there's still the problem of fully funding a retirement plan while having a family that needs every penny you make. You may not be as fortunate as the Mussmans were to sell a family business and net a windfall, but you can still plan for college and save money along the way. Start by cutting down major cost items that are not contributing to improving your family life. These items may range from after-school programs that your kids aren't benefiting from, expensive toys and vacations or camps that don't really further their education. Another less tangible item you need to work on is your own sense of guilt.

When it comes to our children, naturally we want the best in everything and all too often give them a little bit more than what we had as kids. It's the blessing of a new generation. But giving our kids the best isn't the same thing as buying them everything corporate America wants them to have. Remember that the only thing more delicate than a child's hand is a parent's ego. That is part of the madness of modern parenting and it's coming from all directions. When the World War II generation grew up (the parents of baby boomers), there was no *Sesame Street, Barney, Arthur,* computer games, CDs, interactive software, or mass-merchandised kids' movies and TV shows. They had Charlie McCarthy and the occasional classic Disney movie. That was about it. No baby stores, no Toys 'R' Us, just big department stores and single-sponsor radio shows that featured products like Ovaltine.

Is there such a thing as spending too much on our children? While that question will forever be debated, it's important to realize that the single best thing children can have is our loving *attention*. If we don't have balance in our lives, if we are working all the time to buy things we may not need, they get shortchanged, too. Their lives fall out of balance. Their personal ecology—their relationships to you and the outside world—fall out of whack. That's why we need to rebalance our priorities when it comes to our children. That includes everything from the first baby clothes to college.

Balancing Your Family Life Is Part of Any New Prosperity

One measure of prosperity is how well our children are prepared to meet the challenges of the world. The Mussmans made the conscious decision that their family time was more important than building a business. They put family development above wealth creation. The Mussmans wanted their children to know them, share in their appreciation of art, recreation, culture, and where they live. They are preparing them for a world that is undergoing a massive identity crisis. In a broader sense, the Mussmans' new prosperity reflects a deeper preparation for life. If our children are unprepared for the rigors of the world, the future of society is somehow imperiled.

While late-start parents like me are in the minority, you may have children living at home later in life or still need to help them out in adulthood in some way. Can you plan for a new prosperity and provide for your children? Not if your own life is out of balance. Children pick up at an extremely early age their parents' desperation. They'll see it on your faces, but they won't see you most of the time—you'll be too busy working to pay bills. They end up the losers. Of course if you focus on your relationship to the best possible environment for your children, even the daunting matter of funding a six-figure college education becomes possible.

Baby boomers (like myself) often forget what the world was like from 1930 to 1946. No computers. No cell phones. No cable TV. A lot of sacrifice just to buy a 900-square-foot tract home in a suburb after World War II. That's why I have enormous respect for my parents' and their parents' generations. They went from being non-English-speaking immigrants to people surviving a global depression and world war. A pretty tall order that I hope won't be repeated anytime soon. Nevertheless, both earlier generations knew sacrifice and hardship, so they saved and forced the federal government to take care of them when they came back from war (the Veterans Administration and GI Bill) and when they got old (Social Security and Medicare). They told our leaders that in exchange for their sacrifice and hard work, they wanted something in return, so they reaped some of the most beneficial social programs in the history of the republic.

But for those of us under sixty-two, how are we to reap the same benefits? More important, how do we prepare our children, who may take it for granted that they don't have to work until sixty-seven and may have as many as a half-dozen careers in a long life? We work on our own personal ecology. We pursue our goals and reap time for our children because we are balanced in how much we earn and spend. This is new prosperity parenting. The Mussmans had clear goals: Get free of the business, provide an income stream, and move to a place that is family-friendly. Then they would start to work on college funding.

> **NEW PROSPERITY TIP**
>
> The most educational and least expensive trips are right in your community. Take your kids to the fire station, the police station, and public works departments. Most municipal workers will be tickled to give you a tour and tell you how things work. It's 100 percent cheaper than a theme park and you'll get to see your taxes at work.

So let's crack the biggest nut in having a family: paying for college. This is one of the first places where you can apply a sound personal ecology. Balance this situation by asking yourself (and your significant other), How much can we invest while funding our own retirement plans? You can do both if you plan. It wouldn't be fair to your children if you didn't do it this way. If you didn't fully provide for your own retirement, then you might become dependent upon your children. And if they don't receive the education they need, then the reverse may haunt you.

New Prosperity College Planning

Well, this is a big nut, but one that can be cracked a number of ways. It's such a big nut that a lot of parents just throw up their hands when the subject comes up. Based on the present rate of tuition inflation, a public four-year college will cost more than $34,000 a year seventeen years from now; a private college $70,000 a year. That's a whopping $136,000 and $280,000, respectively, for four years. Unlike the consumer price index, the college tuition index keeps soaring at least twice as fast, because (a) parents haven't complained or stopped sending their kids to college, (b) the college degree is still a benchmark for future success and earning power. While *b* may not be the case anymore, *a* is.

Like the retirement arena, the college-planning arena is loaded with funding options. Here are the best strategies:

Save early and often. Use stock-index funds (see step 6) and keep them in your name. Set up a Roth IRA if you'll be at least 59½ when you need the money for college bills.

Set up an education IRA. As mentioned in step 4, the $500 per household contribution isn't much, but you can accumulate more than $20,000 by age seventeen if you start at the child's birth and keep contributing. Again, to get the highest-possible return, invest in low-cost stock index mutual funds.

Take advantage of state college plans. Although it's difficult to make a commitment to send a child to a college in-state when he or she is young, it's a decision that will save you thousands when your child is to go. Most states have a variety of "qualified state tuition savings plans" where you can prepay tuition (and lock in today's tuition rates), buy tax-free bonds (not a very high return), or participate in savings plans. There isn't going to be any state savings program that will allow you to earn stock-market-level returns, so you should employ these programs in addition to your own investment plans with stock index mutual funds. And keep in mind that your child is not guaranteed admission to in-state schools if you participate; he or she still must be accepted.

Consider community colleges. Offered in nearly every county, these wonderful institutions—there are more than 1,100 of them—offer much and cost much less than four-year universities. Community or "junior" colleges may be America's best-kept education secret. Many larger community colleges actually offer more in the way of courses, vocational programs, and basic prerequisites for four-year programs. If your children decide that they want and need a four-year school, they can transfer most of their basic courses and get their degree. Let's face it, basic English, math, and composition courses in the first year of college are pretty much the same at every college, so why pay a fortune for it at an out-of-state school? Another bonus is that your kids can save money by living at home and working. They will have saved something for the rest of their education—and feel great about it—because they will be able to pay for some of their education and possibly save more for a four-year school. You save as well.

When they're in school, take advantage of the Hope Scholarship and Lifetime Learning Credit. As with the education IRA, Congress could have made these tax-related benefits a lot more generous. The Hope Scholarship gives you a tax credit of up to $1,500 per student per year for qualified college expenses like tuition (room and board wouldn't be covered). But you can only use it for the first two years of college (up to sixty credit hours) and eligibility is cut off if your household income is above $100,000 (married, filing jointly) or $50,000 (head of household or single). The Lifetime Learning Credit—which adults can also use—is a one-time credit of $1,000. You can use one or the other of these tax credits, but not both. They both clearly favor the economics of community college.

Apply for financial aid early. And put as much of your children's assets in your name as possible. Colleges typically expect you to contribute no more than 5.65 percent of your assets per year, but 35 percent of your child's assets per year. Another benchmark for aid is the $100,000 per year in household income. Above that most colleges will sniff at your aid application. So if you can defer income the year before you apply for aid or claim a large number of deductions (for self-employment), you may be better off.

Borrow as a last resort. Although you still can obtain student loans at reasonable rates—and pay them off over a long period of time—you may have assets that you didn't know you had. If you have a cash-value life insurance policy and your retirement assets are able to cover life expenses for your survivors upon your demise, cash in the policy or take out a loan against it. Ask your insurance agent for details. Any policy loans don't really have to be paid back, they are just deducted from your "death benefit" (I love this term). You may be able to borrow from your 401(k) or qualified plans at work, but resist the temptation since you'll be sacrificing your own retirement funds and be forced to pay the loans back if you change companies. Home-equity loans are also a consideration and the interest is deductible, but you may not want to have more debt.

Federal government programs. If you do nothing else, fill out a Free Application for Federal Student Aid (FAFSA) form. Every college will provide you with one. It's the master document for a number of federal programs including the Pell grant, Perkins, and Stafford programs. Fill it out the May before your child's first term at school. Work-study programs are also available through this document, but the formulas are complicated, so get a jump start on it.

Campus-based programs. Every college has a number of these. Your child can work in a number of places on campus or qualify for any number of grants. Apply for them through the college's financial aid office.

> **NEW PROSPERITY TIP**
>
> Use the Internet to your advantage to project college costs, locate scholarships, find starting salaries for certain majors, and to download worksheets on financing estimates. See www.nelliemae.com/edvisor or www.jobweb.com.

Scholarships. Apply for these early and apply for every one you possibly can. There are thousands of different sources, so you should check your local library, the Internet, and the colleges you are considering. Also try your employer, state higher-education agencies, foundations, fraternal organizations, ethnic organizations, and college athletic departments.

INFLATION RATES BASED ON TUITION OF $8,990 PER YEAR

Starting Year	Year 2005	Year 2010	Year 2015
Public College			
4%	$13,480	$16,838	$20,486
6%	$17,066	$22,838	$30,562
8%	$20,961	$30,799	$45,254
10%	$25,690	$41,309	$66,528
Private College			
4%	$28,917	$35,182	$42,804
6%	$35,658	$47,718	$63,857
8%	$43,798	$64,353	$86,312
10%	$53,593	$86,312	$139,006

Source: www.dtonline.com (Deloitte and Touche Web site)

Walking Through the College Financing Maze

Your new prosperity plan should include a logical, step-by-step approach to the college-financing labyrinth that starts at the birth of your children, then steps into high gear when they hit the sophomore class in high school. Here's what you need to know:

1. **Estimate the costs of four years of college education in a number of ways.** First, figure two years of a community college, then

two years of a four-year college. Then four years of (a) public four-year school, and (b) private school. With those estimates in hand, have a discussion with your spouse and child on what's doable.

2. **At application time, pull together the "total aid" package.** That means you've applied for every scholarship and know how much you'll pool from your own resources and how much you might borrow. Determine a monthly payment for you and your child in repaying the loans.

3. **Develop an "in-school budget."** How much will your child need for all major expenses, including trips home, books, athletic fees, etc.?

4. **Estimate annual salary and take-home pay for your new graduate, then show him or her how much will be deducted for any loan repayment.** Also show how much you'll be repaying. A good average salary if your graduate hasn't decided on a major is $24,000 a year for a liberal arts/general studies major.

New Prosperity Parenting Strategies

It's ironic, but paying attention to spending is a great way to enhance family life. Even if you don't have children at home, you can employ these spending guidelines to build your new prosperity:

If you have a problem with spending, your kids might, too. Kids see what their parents do and imitate it. If you're in debt all the time, they'll think it's okay. It wouldn't hurt to take another gander at step 2 and get your spending portrait touched up a bit. You are up against a powerful, well-funded banking industry that is putting credit cards into kids' hands at younger and younger ages. According to a Georgetown University study, "About 70 percent of students at four-year colleges have at least one credit card, and revolving debt on these cards averages more than $2,000." That's an alarming statistic that you can nip in the bud by paying cash for as much as you can now and saving for the things you need—and make sure your children see you doing it.

Start early and teach your children how to save. My daughter Sarah had a bank before she turned one. I know that sounds strange, but we had a lot of fun teaching her how to put money in it and learning the difference between Mr. Lincoln and Mr. Jefferson. As I mentioned, we also set up Roth IRAs to jump-start her college fund the year she was born and an Education IRA (see step 4 for details). By her second year, she had more than $4,500 in her college fund (we'll be able to tap my Roth, but not my wife Kathleen's without penalty). We are funding these vehicles with low-cost stock-index funds.

Clothes are expensive, so network within your family. My niece Arianna Eve is about a year older than Sarah and my daughter inherited a lot of clothes from her. Children's clothes have gotten very expensive, but you don't have to pay top dollar for them. All of the clothes, however, are made in the same place no matter what the label says. They are the same whether they are bought at Toys 'R' Us, Wal Mart, or the neighborhood thrift store. They'll grow out of them, so you won't even have to like them or worry about quality.

Put dollar limits on what you buy. I know this is extremely hard to do, but I've seen dads buy motorized plastic cars for their kids to ride around in costing hundreds of dollars. Children really don't know the difference between an inexpensive toy and a pricey one—unless we insist on telling them. Tell grandparents the same thing. If you really want to spoil your kids, give them a financially secure life. Instead of birthday parties where the gifts outnumber the kids, tell parents to bring college-fund contributions. Later on, give them a choice of a single item they can buy with the money they've saved. Since they only have so much money, they'll realize that there are limits to their spending power, which is a lesson that is best learned early in life.

Don't shop impulsively; make lists, check them twice. Who cares who's naughty or nice? When you make lists and comparison shop, you don't go crazy and buy everything you think your kids will like. If they like books, buy them books. If they like trains, indulge them, but give them a chance to enjoy them. So many kids are buried in toys. They can only play with one at a time.

If you're expecting (or your children are), do some pre-birth planning. A startling number, but it's estimated that raising a child from birth to age seventeen will cost $115,020 plus tax. At least that's what the U.S. Department of Agriculture claims for a family making less than $36,000 per year. For those making more than $60,000 annually, the per-child total nearly doubles to $228,690. If you read between the lines, you can easily conclude that the more you make, the more you spend—on your children. But spending more on them won't make them any smarter or better equipped to deal with the world. The more debt you're in, the more they'll be in debt as well. So put aside the savings you need on a regular basis by setting up automatic withdrawals from your checking account into a money market mutual fund (see step 8).

Quick and Powerful Ways to Save on Children-Related Expenses

Setting up college funds is but one part of planning for kids. Will you still have two incomes when you start a family (if you are still pondering it)? It may make more sense for one spouse to stay at home. Quality day care is expensive, often the third-costliest item in your budget after your mortgage and car payment. And working becomes less lucrative for the lower-earning spouse because you still have to consider the costs of getting to work, dry cleaning, lunches, and unreimbursed business expenses. Plan ahead and save. Here are some bargains you can find:

1. Shop around on the Internet. You can buy nearly everything and save time and money. There's lots of kids' stuff. Use some of the search engines in the Resources section at the back of this book to find everything from bikes to xylophones.

2. Skip any product that involves licensing. I have nothing against Pooh, Barney, Arthur, or Sesame Street toys. You will pay more for these products because the cost of advertising and merchandising them is built into the purchase price. And if your child doesn't live for these characters, there's no reason you should pay extra for them.

3. Buy books used and unlicensed. Kids' books have gotten too expensive as well, although they haven't changed over the years. As with other products, you pay more for the licensed merchandise and feel like you're locked in to similar products if your child likes them. Fortunately, books are plentiful at garage sales, library sales, thrift shops, and rummage sales.

4. Shop thrift and outlet stores. This is a great place to find children's furniture, one of the biggest rip-offs on the planet. Besides, kids tend to treat their furniture badly up until a certain age and it depreciates rapidly.

5. Skip formula if you can. If you have the flexibility, breast-feeding is still the best thing for infants. You can save more than $500 by doing it. Formula is more expensive than most good wines.

6. Skip expensive vacations. I know this is heresy to the Las Vegas and Orlando tourism bureaus, but kids derive just as much pleasure going to a local park, flying a kite, and being with you when you are relaxed and having fun than getting on a plane and spending their time being shuttled around to amusement parks. Camping is also meaningful and inexpensive. Most of my summers were spent exploring the vast landscape from coast to coast. I've seen forty-eight states, most of those with my parents and brothers. You'll save thousands and teach your kids a lot about this incredible planet of ours, because they'll see it firsthand and not in some virtual-reality ride.

7. Need a bigger house for the children? Add on. If you're happy with the local school district, add the rooms you need to your home. By moving to a newer house, you may improve one or two aspects of your life, but lose a little prosperity in the trade. Bigger homes mean higher taxes, more maintenance, higher utility bills, and the life-energy you and your spouse are going to consume in working to pay for it. Your children need your time. Love provides all the space in the world they will ever need.

8. Take advantage of free activities in your community. They are usually of high quality and going on all the time. Start with your library. Most public libraries have storytelling hours, activity rooms, and concerts. Also check out community centers, holiday concerts, park districts, and colleges. In most metropolitan areas, there's a wide spectrum of cultural events.

9. Grow your own, get your kids involved early. It's not true that kids don't like a variety of foods. You can provide them with a good lesson in self-sufficiency and a diverse, nutritional low-sugar diet just by tending your garden. Have your children dig and pull weeds alongside you. They'll love it, because kids have a magnetic attraction to dirt. Freeze or can what you grow in the summer; if you live deep in the Sun Belt, you'll have a year-round pantry in your backyard. You'll be teaching them respect for the earth at an early age and they'll thank you for it later, because they'll have a healthy diet for life.

10. Turn off the television as much as you possibly can. TV is the most efficient advertising delivery vehicle ever created. It puts advertising directly into our brains; it's more efficient than an intravenous injection. And all the time TV is pounding those millions of messages of what to buy, we're being demeaned by ideas that we're not good enough, smart enough, sexy enough, or rich enough. No wonder kids have problems developing a healthy self-esteem. They're constantly being told they're worthless unless they buy that video game, bike, skateboard, or toy. A home without an active television set promotes active minds because TV is a passive activity that promotes sitting. My family only watches broadcast television once a year together, and that's for the president's state of the union speech. The rest of the time we leave the tube off and sing, dance, read, play videos, the radio, the piano, or CDs. It's improved our marriage, our daughter hasn't missed it, and we don't structure our lives around TV shows. We also don't have cable or satellite and will never have it. If you do nothing else, consider this one move. It will change your life and help your children immensely. Everyone thinks we're strange, but our daughter is happy. We also talk out problems each evening instead of being captive to a favorite TV show or cable movie. Although we still have heated discussions, there is no distraction to our reverie.

Kids: Summary of Our Future

1. Be a good example by keeping your spending and savings balanced, then teach your children well about how to save and spend wisely.

2. Use every possible college savings plan available, and consider state schools and community colleges for at least the first two years of college.

3. Spend time with your kids, turn off the TV, and take experiential vacations.

4. Save money by avoiding overpriced kids' merchandise. Shop for quality not labels.

Making Your Money Last as Long as You Do

"You can be young without money, but you can't be old without it."
—Tennessee Williams

As a cyber guru on early retirement, John Greaney is preaching from his Web pulpit to the entire world. There's little he doesn't know or hasn't researched about the subject of leaving the workforce before age sixty-five. He's calculated things like projecting safe withdrawal rates from your IRAs to finding programs that show you the rate of inflation on your investments over time. If he hasn't crunched the numbers, nobody has. On his Retire Early Home Page, you can see his handiwork. This is a man who loves to see the power of numbers working for you, and he knows every angle.

For a forty-three-year-old, he's been more places than a sailor, and he knew early in his career as a civil engineer that corporate life was not for him. So at twenty-five he planned his exit strategy; he had worked for companies like Exxon, TRW, and Ogden Corporation. In November of 1994, while working for a chemical company in Baton Rouge, although he was single, thirty-eight, and making $85,000 a year, he left the workforce for good with a $500,000 nest egg, a move that shocked even his mother at the time. Unless something extraordinary happens, "I'd have to be virtually homeless before I'd go back.

"I didn't wanted to be working a job I hated when I was forty or fifty," Greaney proudly notes, and admits "I'm still living [as cheaply as] a college student."

These days, in addition to running the best early-retirement Web site on the Internet, he plays golf two to three times a week and does some engineering consulting, "But only if like the company." The rest of the time he's relaxing, enjoying the company of his dog, Lupo, and managing his investment portfolio, which affords him a great deal of security in his rented apartment in Houston. Since he's lived all over the country, he prefers Houston because its cost of living is less than one-third of either coast and health care is reasonably priced, so much so that he would have paid double the premium on his health plan in his home state of Connecticut.

Although he lives a modest lifestyle, John insists that any person who does the homework can retire early if they keep in mind some fundamentals:

- Since he's no longer covered by his last employer's health plan, John purchased a policy through a professional engineering group and notes that professional associations are good sources for group policies. He pays $220 a month for a Preferred Provider Organization (a group of doctors, clinics, and hospitals) that includes major medical and dental coverage.

- He lives modestly and doesn't plan to buy a new car or house anytime soon because he's happy with what he has. "I don't like cutting the lawn or shoveling snow." If he wanted to, he could easily afford either since his nest egg has grown to some $2.5 million.

- He likes to keep one to two years of living expenses in cash, most of it in a money market mutual fund and the rest to cover five years' worth of expenses in U.S. Treasury bonds or high-yielding FDIC-insured CDs in varying maturities, a practice known as "laddering."

- By employing the IRS's 72 (t) exemption (see step 3), he's begun to withdraw funds from his IRA without incurring penalties. He's trying to keep his annual withdrawal rate safely below 4% and is confident his money will last for forty years, although he qualifies that calculation by saying, "If we have a repeat of the crash of 1929, I expect my money to last for forty years. If the crash of 1929 doesn't reoccur and I live to be ninety, I expect to have more money than a ninety-year-old could efficiently spend."

- John has 92% of his total retirement portfolio in stocks or stock mutual funds. Single issues include Dell, Pfizer, Servicemaster, Lilly, and Cendant. All told, he has about a dozen stocks diversified across several industries for lower risk.

- Owning housing is a bad deal for him as long as the stock market returns around 12% a year and inflation is under 5% a year. Besides, John doesn't want to worry about maintenance concerns and likes it when the manager fixes the air conditioning in his apartment.

Insulating and Sustaining Your New Prosperity Portfolio

The best way to manage money is to pretend it's a sea tortoise: it's slow, gets where its going, and lives a long time if it's on the right path. Your money will work for you, but you need to do some homework to see that you won't outlast its ability to provide for you. As the following table illustrates, you could be living a long time. But one of the greatest fears of all retirees is that they will outlive their money. After all, if the odds are 78 percent you'll make it to age eighty (65 percent odds for men), you have to ensure that your money is still growing for several decades past your retirement. So if you're able to retire at fifty, you may be looking at another thirty to fifty years of investing.

You may live to be more than a hundred years old. But if you're leaving the workforce early, you need to do everything possible to see that you don't outlive your money. A couple of safeguards will ensure the longevity of your prosperity funds. If you do the planning now, you won't regret it later.

LIVE LONG AND PROSPER: THE PROBABILITY OF SURVIVING BEYOND AGE 65

Future Age	Female	Male
70	96%	92%
75	89%	81%
80	78%	65%
90	40%	26%
95	19%	11%
100	6%	3%

Source: Society of Actuaries

Safe Withdrawal Rates: What You Need to Know

If your money won't last as long as you do, will you take a job when you're ninety? I know that sounds ridiculous, but it may happen if your new prosperity portfolio isn't sustainable. A delicate relationship exists between the money you withdraw, your total return, and the diversification of your investments. Like an internal-combustion engine, if one factor is imbalanced, you'll come up short later on. Here's how safe withdrawal works in principle:

1. If you take out too much money every year, you will erode the principal, or the core of your funds. The higher your annual withdrawal rate, the faster your funds will be depleted.

2. The lower the return of your overall portfolio, the less chance your funds will be growing more than your withdrawal rate. If you're not making up the funds you withdraw every year, that contributes to depletion of your assets, most notably your principal.

3. If the mix of your investments doesn't focus primarily on growth, then that's also a big negative for sustainability. Although mixing bonds with stocks is okay, the dominant investment should be stocks. Remember, you also need to beat inflation in addition to outpacing your withdrawal rate. A half-stocks, half-bond mix probably won't do it for you over time; at least 60 percent in stocks is a far more potent growth mixture—even in early retirement.

Fortunately, you can take some simple steps with your planning that will avoid premature depletion of your funds. A solid body of academic research shows what are the most likely "safe" rates of withdrawal, rate of return, and asset mix. Based on stock market data from Prof. Robert Shiller of Yale University, John Greaney has calculated what's doable in terms of withdrawal rates.

SAFE "ZONES" FOR WITHDRAWAL RATES

Pay Out Period	10 Yrs	20 Yrs	30 Yrs	40 Yrs	50 Yrs
% Stocks in Fund	44%	66%	71%	77%	82%
Investment Expenses	.20%	.20%	.20%	.20%	.20%
Max. Withdrawal Rate*	7.56%	4.75%	3.81%	3.54%	3.37%

*100% "safe" withdrawal rate adjusted for inflation. This study is based on a $1,000 initial portfolio.

Source: John Greaney, Retire Early Home Page (www.geocities.com/wallstreet/8257)

It's clear that the higher percentage of stocks you hold in a port-folio, the more likely your money will survive over a long period of time. The 0.20% investment expense ratio is also a factor because, as I've mentioned in earlier chapters, investment expenses will reduce your total return over time. You can find 0.20% on the largest stock-index funds. The maximum withdrawal rate recom-mended here drops the longer you'll need your money. If you aver-age the various withdrawal rates in this study, an average rate of withdrawal of 4.6% is probably a modest approach to the amount you can safely cash out each year and maintain enough to live on for another forty years or so. Limiting your withdrawals to this rate means that—based on data collected from 1871 to 1998—there was no period in which you would have exhausted your retirement funds.

Safe Withdrawal Prosperity Tips

- You'll need stocks as more than half of your new prosperity port-folio to beat inflation. For even more long-term growth, consider investing from 60% to 80% in stocks, growing at an average annual return of at least 8%.

- Once you get higher than the 7% per year withdrawal rate, your money may not last. Try not to withdraw the principal of your new prosperity funds; make sure you're tapping cash and non-tax-deferred assets first.

- Keeping investment expenses low is also critical in maintaining a safe withdrawal rate. That's why low-cost index funds are ideal long-term vehicles for your new prosperity portfolio. If you have mutual funds that are charging you more than 0.25% per year in expenses, then you can always roll them over into the index funds recommended in step 6.

- You can lower expenses and boost returns even more by building a diversified stock portfolio (see step 6). John Greaney says that he's paying less than $100 per year in fees to maintain his portfolio. He estimates he'd pay $3,000 to $4,000 a year if he had all of his

retirement funds in the Vanguard S&P Index Fund. Of course, index funds are still the way to go if you don't feel comfortable researching and picking stocks.

RISK AND ALLOCATION (1926-1997)

Stock/Bond Allocation (%)*	Number of Years with a Loss	Average One-Year Loss (%)	Three-Year Loss (%) 1930–1932	Two-Year Loss (%) 1973–1974
100/0	20	–12.3	–60.9	–37.3
80/20	19	–9.8	–45.6	–29.2
60/40	16	–8.2	–30.2	–21.1
40/60	15	–5.5	–14.9	–13.0
20/80	14	–3.7	+0.5	–4.9

*Allocations are not rebalanced annually.

Source: The Vanguard Group

Choosing the Right Distribution Option

Let's say it's time for you to take your pension, whether it's part of an early-retirement plan or not. You have a choice as to how you receive the money. The way you choose your distribution will ultimately affect how much money is available for you from it—and your loved one. If you make the wrong decision, it may haunt you. These are the most commonly used options:

Lump sum. In this case, the company hands over a big pile of money to you at one time from a defined-contribution plan. You can spend it or "roll it over" directly into an IRA vehicle of your choice. If you spend it, you're looking at a tremendous (and unnecessary) tax hit because you'll pay a 10% penalty (if made before 59½) and income tax. Say your company buys you out and basically hands you your $300,000 401(k) balance, which they are

legally obligated to do. Taking the money as cash triggers a $30,000 penalty plus $84,000 in nominal taxes if you're in the 28% marginal bracket; you're left with $186,000. Any bank, mutual fund, or brokerage house will accept a rollover. This would save you a lot of heartache later because if you don't do a rollover within sixty days of receipt of the money, the government will automatically withhold 20% of the sum. Do you like the idea of the IRS sitting on $60,000 of your money without paying you a dime in interest? If you handle the distribution correctly, you'll pay only ordinary income tax when you receive it monthly payments later on.

Single life. You will receive your defined-benefit pension as a fixed monthly payment for the rest of your life. When you die, it stops and so does the money. A good choice if you have no survivors or if your spouse has a pension; then you'll reap the highest monthly payment.

Term certain. A reduced monthly annuity will be paid for a guaranteed period of time such as ten or fifteen years.

Joint and survivor. You and your spouse will be covered, but the surviving spouse receives a smaller percentage (from 10% to 15% lower) of the benefit. A good way to cover the surviving spouse, but clearly not the most generous. Initial payments are smaller than the single option, so you may want to see what other assets can cover your spouse (such as other IRAs) so that you can maximize your distribution by choosing this option.

The Fallback Part of Your Portfolio: Secure Cash Management

Since you're probably painfully aware of how much you spend and earn each month by now, you need a good place to put that short-term money that isn't the core of your retirement kitty. As with all your other investments—and these are just holding vehicles for cash—you'll need the lowest-cost vehicles that give you the highest possible income. These vehicles should hold no more than 20 per-

cent of your total assets and be able to cover at least a year's worth of living expenses, plus any "extra" items like travel or new cars.

Money market mutual funds. The core of any solid cash-management plan has to include money-market mutual funds because the best funds track short-term interest rates by investing in commercial paper and government obligations with short maturities. Generally, the higher the amount on deposit, the better the rate of return. The most aggressively marketed funds are waiving management fees, so you get a slightly higher return. Although you'll barely beat the return on one-year U.S. government bonds, your principal is secure in a money fund and the yield will track short-term rates. Your money is always available by writing a check or making an electronic funds transfer. Unlike certificates of deposit, you can get at your money any time and you will be able to track rises in interest rates. The two best sources are *Barron's* or www.ibcdata.com.

U.S. Treasury bills and notes. You can buy them from the U.S. Bureau of Public Debt through the "Treasury Direct" program at no commission and have the interest automatically deposited into an account of your choice. "Ladder" the maturities from one to five years in maturity to give you diversification. See the Treasury's fine Web site (www.ustreas.gov) for all the details. U.S. bonds are for money you don't need right away but may need in a few years for short-term or living expenses.

I-Bonds. These relatively new Treasury bonds will track the Consumer Price Index plus pay you the market rate of return. You buy them through the Treasury or Bureau of Public Debt. They are worthwhile additions to the cash portion of your portfolio, but you don't buy them for growth.

Buying the Insurance You Need

Most people avoid the subject of insurance about as much as they can. But it's a "what if" kind of planning decision that needs to be done before you can call your new prosperity plan complete. You may feel that you have adequate insurance on all fronts, but let's take a look at it anyway.

You should review every one of your policies because you can save thousands in policy premiums over time. You can "self-insure" and save on nearly every policy if you do some comparison shopping. Self-insurance is the amount that you can afford to pay out of pocket on any given policy, whether it's health, home, or auto. The universal rule is that the more you self-insure, the higher your *deductible* on the policy and the more you will save. Each time you choose a low or no-deductible policy, you are saying that you *can't* afford any loss on that particular insured item. If you're in a position to retire early, that's unlikely to be the case. Let's say you're reviewing your homeowners policy and you have a $250 deductible. By raising the deductible to $1,000, you'll bank an extra few hundred dollars a year, depending on the insurer. That gives you more cash. Keep in mind that you can do that with nearly any policy to lower a premium.

Health insurance. This would be an individual policy you would need to purchase for you *or your spouse* if your employer didn't offer post-retirement coverage. As I mentioned in step 3, federal law prohibits refusal of coverage for "preexisting conditions." In the real world, however, insurers can jack up your premiums if you've had any number of surgeries, ailments, chronic or acute conditions. My mother, for example, had to buy an extremely expensive individual plan at $6,000 a year with a $3,000 deductible when my father retired (until she qualified for Medicare in 1999) that restricted coverage on breasts and other organs. If an insurer considers you high risk—that is, you've had a serious malady like heart disease, cancer, or a major chronic ailment—you'll be bounced into the highest-premium categories. In that instance, you may need to take a huge deductible of $1,000 or more just to afford the premium. A recent U.S. General Accounting Office report noted that "high-risk individuals and some small groups may continue to face high premiums for guaranteed coverage because HIPAA [Health Insurance Portability and Accountability Act, a federal law prohibiting discrimination against the insured with preexisting conditions] does not constrain carriers' rating practices beyond existing state laws." Most large states have "high-risk" pools that allow you to purchase policies if you are in this category at affordable group rates, but these are last resorts. It is possible to save money by excluding certain conditions (heart disease, cancer, etc.) that bump you into high-risk pricing, but you are taking a chance that way if one of these conditions recurs. Nevertheless, get quotes from as many insurers as you can and even consider a managed-care plan if choice of doctors is not a problem. Also contact any organizations you've belonged to over the years to see if they offer group coverage. That includes alumni, fraternal, professional, trade, and business organizations. Many people find the most affordable premium that way.

Disability. Even though you are considering early retirement, you may need this insurance if you plan to reenter the workforce or if your new prosperity plan is dependent upon taking alternative employment such as contract work, consulting, or other jobs that might involve more than thirty hours of your time. Disability plans cover you for a certain period of time if you become disabled and can't work. In your working life, you are more likely to need and use disability coverage than life coverage, which only pays your survivors a death benefit. Most life insurers offer disability coverage. It's also available through professional associations and through Internet quote services.

Homeowners/renters insurance. You probably already know that your policy should have an inflation rider in it that will automatically cover the rising cost of your home and contents. It should also reflect what you own, any improvements to the home, and where you live. If you live in a particularly litigious area, it wouldn't hurt to purchase a $1 million "umbrella liability" rider. This covers a range of things that people might sue you over from a fall on an icy sidewalk to a mishap on a bike. Make sure that it's worth the money, however. If the policy has more exclusions than covered items, it may be a waste of money. As I mentioned before, increase your deductible for maximum savings. There are also discounts for smoke detectors and alarm and sprinkler systems. As with the other policy quotes you obtain, start with your present insurer first. They may be able to find you discounts just to keep your business, especially if you threaten to take several policies elsewhere. There are also reasonable discounts for keeping your homeowners and auto policies all with one company. Be sure to ask for them; agents may not readily volunteer this information.

Vehicle insurance. Most people pay too much when it comes to this coverage. There are more ways to save than any other kind of insurance, but agents are loath to volunteer the information. The latest safety equipment, for example, always garners the most reliable discounts. Generally older, less desirable (to steal) cars are cheaper to insure than newer, fancier cars. You do best if you have a car that's over five years old, is paid for, and you don't care if it gets banged up a little. Keep in mind you can drop comprehensive (theft, non-collision damage) and collision coverage altogether. If the "book" value of your car is low enough (check out www. kbb.com), you probably don't need coverage for anything except liability, which can't be dropped. When I got into the last years of owning my 1988 Acura Integra, for example, I dropped the comprehensive coverage and raised the collision deductible to $1,000. I was saving more than $100 a year that way. I didn't care if a tree fell on it, and nobody was going to steal a car that old. As with all other forms of insurance, the higher the deductibles, the more money you save. Where you live is also a factor, especially if you are planning to relocate. If you live in a city, for example, your rates are usually higher than if you live in a suburb or the country, where theft rates are dramatically lower. So keep in mind that any lifestyle change may impact your auto insurance premiums.

Long-term care insurance. This is one of the hazards of getting older. Not only do you start to be concerned about your health, but you're keeping a close eye on your parents as well. Due to changes in longevity, you're going to see a lot more children taking care of parents. The number of one-hundred-year-olds doubled in 1998— to 700,000. There's going to be more than one million centenari-

DON'T IGNORE LONG-TERM CARE COSTS

Projection for long-term care, including home and nursing-home care, in billions.

| | 2000 | 2010 | 2020 | 2030 | 2040 |

Percentage of overall long-term care payment for the elderly.

Out of pocket payments by individual or families	39.0%
Medicaid	31.4%
Medicare	25.0%
Other federal programs	2.6%
Other state and local programs	1.2%
Long-term care insurance	0.8%

Source: U.S. House Ways and Means Committee

ans in the next century and they just might be your parents (or you, God willing). Unfortunately, our social welfare system hasn't been updated adequately to care for the extremely old (a subject I've explored in depth in my investigative writing at *Consumers Digest*). You'll need to probe the costs of long-term care for your parents—and yourself. For starters, not everyone who reaches their eighties ends up in a nursing home, but here are a few facts that are real eye-openers:

LONG-TERM CARE FACTS

- For the eighty-five-and-older group, the assistance rate (those who need help) with activities of daily living is more than 20%.

- By 2015, some 3.2 million Americans will have Alzheimer's disease and 1.7 million will need personal assistance.

- Family members provide up to 90% of all long-term care assistance, most of it in the form of caregiving in the home.

■ The average American man will need $56, 895 of long-term care during his lifetime; women (who generally live longer than men) will need $124,370.

■ Nursing-home bills can easily exceed $50,000 a year in some areas. Medicare pays for only twenty days of skilled nursing care and nothing for unskilled or "custodial" care.

(Source: "The Crisis in Long-Term Care," *Consumers Digest* magazine, May/June 1998, also available at www.consumersdigest.com. Click under "Issues and Investigations.")

There are a number of ways to prepare for long-term care expenses that will insulate your new prosperity plan. You can approach this topic cautiously at a later date, but now is the best time, since any surprise expenses may adversely impact your early retirement.

1. **Talk with your parents.** Would they have enough assets to cover a nursing home stay for either one of them? Do they have long-term care insurance? Would they consider it?

2. **Price a long-term care insurance plan.** For policyholders under sixty-five, these are fairly affordable; after that age the premiums skyrocket. They are also complicated and not recommended if your parents have assets in excess of $1 million and the at-home spouse could afford to live comfortably while the other spouse was in a nursing home.

3. **Consider community resources.** Long-term care services in the community have come a long way in recent years and continue to expand. Most metropolitan areas have special apartments for senior citizens that may offer assistance services. There are also assisted living facilities, adult day care, home nursing, homemaking and related services, and a wide range of options that don't include nursing homes. Consider retirement apartments, congregate (group) housing, and several variations on senior housing that are cropping up in every community.

4. **Would your parents consider a reverse mortgage to pay for long-term care expenses?** This is possible if they've paid off all or most of their mortgage. Essentially a bank calculates the equity in the home and pays the occupants a monthly payment based on how much the home is worth. They get paid as long as they live in the house and the bank gets the house when they die. It's a reasonable alternative to provide money for long-term care, but should be considered carefully because the home will not pass into an estate upon your parents' passing—the bank will take it.

5. **How much would the family (your siblings and other relatives) help out in a long-term care situation?** How much would your siblings, cousins, aunts, and uncles help out? Do they live close enough to be of assistance? If one or both of your parents needed care for an extended period of time, are there alternatives within your community that your family would have access to in a short period of time?

6. **Do you have a long-term care policy option through work?** Many employers are now offering group rates on long-term care for employees and parents of employees. If this is offered to you, see if you can continue the coverage at the group rates.

Life insurance. Although the insurance industry makes life insurance sound essential, it's really not. First of all, life insurance is not a retirement plan. Your family—not you—reaps the full benefits only if the Grim Reaper reaps you. You only need it if you don't have enough funds to cover your dependents' expenses upon your demise. Remember, this is not something you could fully use in your lifetime, except if you have *cash-value* insurance, which is costly to buy. By the way, if you do have a cash-value policy and your dependents' financial needs are covered, either cash it in and invest the money or take out a loan against it if you want to keep the policy in force. If you decide you need life insurance, then purchase a *term-life* policy for a fixed period of time. This is a "pure" insurance policy that only provides a *death benefit* (a lump sum of money when you die) and no gimmicky savings or investment components, which are almost always bad investments because the fees are so high. See quoting services in the box below to obtain the best premium prices.

Medigap. Also called the "Medicare supplement," this policy covers what Medicare doesn't, except for long-term care (which have their own policies). You won't have to worry about buying Medigap until you reach sixty-two. The best reason to have it is to cover prescription benefits, unless Congress finds a way to cover that often costly part of health care before you hit that age. You can also choose Medigap plans that cover deductibles on parts A and B (medical services and hospital care) and other less onerous items. They are well worth the money for the drug coverage alone, particularly if you have a chronic condition and need constant medication. Also consider a Medicare HMO if being restricted to the HMO's choice of doctors is not a problem.

Insurance to avoid. There are any number of ways that insurance is passed off as an essential part of your financial plan. The following policies should be avoided because they are incredibly overpriced and a waste of money.

- **Credit-life insurance.** This little policy is tacked on to mortgages and car loans. The insurer will generously cover your outstanding debts at an outrageously high premium upon your demise. If you already have life insurance, this policy is unneeded.

- **Rental car insurance.** If you have a policy on your own car, it will cover a rental car. Rental car companies love to sell you collision damage plans because they make lots of money on them.

- **Dental insurance.** Most dental plans cover large, expensive procedures; routine exams, cleanings, and fillings won't even clear the deductible. If you can continue group plan coverage at a reasonable rate, do so, but individual plans don't cover much at all, so avoid them.

- **Disease insurance.** Major medical plans cover all diseases and conditions, so there's no reason to buy special coverage.

- **Flight insurance.** Airline fatalities are among the rarest events in the modern world; you're more likely to die in your bathtub or from heart disease. Don't buy it.

- **Life insurance on your children.** This is just another way of padding an insurance agent's pocket. Unless your children are breadwinners, they don't need to be covered.

- **Credit card loss/theft insurance.** Under federal law, if your credit card is lost or stolen, you have to pay only $50 on new charges, sometimes not even that much. Also avoid "credit card registration" services. Keep a list of cards at home or just hang on to the old bills. Better yet, just keep one card and all of the bills—review them carefully each month.

> **NEW PROSPERITY TIP**
>
> The best way of buying life, health, Medicare-supplement, and auto insurance is over the Internet. So called "quote" services will survey hundreds of companies and pull up the lowest quotes available. Some prime quote services are
> www.quotesmith.com,
> www.selectquote.com,
> www.directquote.com,
> www.term-quote.com.

- **Contact lens insurance; appliance insurance.** These are simply not worth the money.

Sustaining Your Nest Egg: Getting Help

The best way to protect your new prosperity portfolio is to admit what you don't know and learn about it, or hire someone who does. Although most early-retirement planning is accessible to most people, it's certainly not for everyone. You may need some help. The most difficult part is making your prosperity portfolio sustainable, that is, making it last for as long as you and your significant other live. But factoring in inflation, taxes, rates of return, investment mix, and withdrawal rates is no picnic. It's best done with software (see Resources at the end of the book) or with the help of a financial planner.

Brokers may call themselves "financial advisors," but all they're interested in is making a commission. They don't care a whit about how your investments perform. The best appellation I've seen is a "financial consultant." Sure they consult—on how to take as much of your money as they can, usually by selling stocks, bonds, options, and commodities. You should avoid planners who are also brokers who sell you products while recommending them.

Financial planners come in all stripes and go by a number of different titles. True financial planners are *certified* financial planners; that is, they have gone through a two-year curriculum that teaches them about taxes, portfolio management, and a host of other issues. There are many financial professionals, however, who claim to provide financial planning but may not have the expertise you need. Always review their credentials before hiring them (see checklist below).

The most objective advice is compensated on a flat-fee or hourly basis through "fee-only" financial planners who charge only for their time. What kind of planner you choose will ultimately depend on what kind of services you need. Planners may specialize or offer an array of services, ranging from estate planning to tax preparation, portfolio management, and investment planning. These services may be offered by one person or spread out in the larger planning firms among specialists.

The following is a checklist of suggestions for how to find a competent and trustworthy financial planner:

✔ Interview more than one planner in your area, preferably fee-only planners.

✔ Ask how they are compensated. They may be on salary or a combination fee and commission. If they are fee-only, ask them for a flat rate if you know what you want. Get an estimate of how much it would cost to implement what you plan to do.

✔ Have set objectives before you approach any planner. Do you want them to evaluate an early-retirement plan? Do your taxes? Manage your money? The more you want them to do, the more it will cost you. Pick out the things you know you can't or won't do and get quotes on those services.

✔ Find out what areas they specialize in or provide through other professionals. Do they perform estate/tax planning in addition to retirement planning? Do they have an in-house portfolio manager, or will they place you in no-load mutual funds?

✔ Ask them to describe their background, work history, and credentials. At the minimum, they should be *certified financial planners*. If they manage money, they should be *registered investment advisors* and provide a "Form ADV" that they file with the S.E.C. If they choose investments, they should also be *certified financial analysts*. If they handle taxes, it's preferable—but not required—that they be *certified public accountants*. In estate-planning specialties, a Juris Doctor or law degree is helpful. Helpful but not required credentials for financial planning are degrees in finance and administration. If planners you interview sell securities or insurance, they should be licensed in your state.

✔ Are the planners you interview primarily insurance salespeople or brokers for certain financial products? If so, how much commission would they make on each product they recommend and how would it reduce your total return? Planners carrying the designations *Chartered Life Underwriters/ Chartered Financial Consultants* are trained to sell you life insurance products, although they may have other planning skills as well.

✔ Do they have any business affiliation with other professionals or other financial service providers? Are they compensated for recommending other professionals or products? How much?

✔ Do they provide a written *client engagement agreement* outlining their services? They should. Read it and understand it. If there's something you don't comprehend, ask.

✔ If there is a dispute, how will it be resolved? Will you agree to an arbitration clause in your client agreement?

✔ If they manage money, what is their audited performance for the last five years? How does it compare to the appropriate "benchmark index" for the kinds of stocks/bonds they are managing? Keep in mind most private money managers do not consistently beat indexes, so be wary of high-performance claims. Their performance should be audited by an independent firm.

✓ Has the planner or any principal in the firm been disciplined, sued, or sanctioned by clients? Use the resources that follow to check their claims.

✓ Will the planner work directly with you or refer you to associates? If you will be working with associates, how much training do they have and what are their specialties?

✓ Can they provide references? How many clients do they have? Check out all references.

✓ Ask them to outline their approach to planning. If they immediately recommend an investment or course of action, leave as soon as possible. On your second meeting, describe your objectives and ask them to propose a complete plan with cost estimate.

Financial Planning Resources

TO LOCATE A PLANNER IN YOUR AREA

National Association of Personal Financial Advisors, 888-FEE-ONLY

Institute of Certified Financial Planners, 800-282-PLAN

International Association for Financial Planning, 888-806-PLAN

American Institute of Certified Public Accountants, 800-862-4272

TO CHECK THE DISCIPLINARY HISTORY OF A PLANNER/ADVISOR

North American Securities Administrators Association, 888-84-NASAA

National Association of Securities Dealers, 800-289-9999

National Fraud Exchange, 800-822-0416

Securities and Exchange Commission, 800-732-0330

Certified Financial Planner Board of Standards, 888-CFP-MARK

National Association of Insurance Commissioners, 816-842-3600

Insulate and Sustain

1. Make sure you have the right mix of investments, with a sustainable rate of return and withdrawal rate, to ensure the longevity of your money.

▩

2. Understand the different lump-sum options in your company plans. Use the ones that guarantee the most amount of money to cover your needs.

▩

3. Build up cash accounts with liquid income investments. Try to maintain them and use them through your first and second years in retirement.

▩

4. Know how much and what kinds of insurance you need. Pare back the policies and raise deductibles to save even more money.

▩

5. If you need help, get help, but hire a planner who is selling advice, not products.

Finding a Full Life after Leaving Full-Time Work Behind

Who we really are is bigger than all the attributes of the world,
whether in terms of fame or fortune. Who we are is more than our race,
nationality, class, gender, political affiliation, or club membership.
                                                    —Rev. Robert Aguirre

Some of Dr. Margaret Hellie-Huyck's friends are retiring early. And after a thirty-year career as researcher, teacher, and writer, she can certainly follow them. Her investments have done well, her two daughters are off pursuing careers or postgraduate study, and there's little she says she needs to accomplish in her career. Although she's sixty, she looks forty-five as she sips on a beer while I drink my coffee. It's clear both her career and her volunteer work with the Older Women's League integrate into a satisfying whole, a unity that she prefers to keep intact for a while.

"I could easily spend all my time writing and volunteering, but I haven't reached the tipping point yet." She smiles. For most of us, the "tipping point" is that bifurcation in life when the conventional workforce has little to offer us and the rest of our lives—that other life we need to lead—beckons. Although there are many wise words that will emerge from Margaret's pen in the years to come, she wants to wait. Her husband, Tom, though self-employed as a lawyer, doesn't have a company pension plan. So a few more years investing in the teachers retirement system (TIAA-CREF) won't hurt. It's a flexible kind of plan that will ensure their financial security because she is contributing the maximum allowed.

Although it was unusual in 1965, Margaret and Tom have lived extremely modestly and have reaped the benefits. They bought their apartment condominium for $12,500 in Chicago's sophisticated Hyde Park neighborhood and still live there. They own and drive a 1986 Toyota Corolla with 125,000 miles on it. Early on in their marriage they decided not to "go suburban" and to stay in the city. Tom was usually home by 5:30 P.M. and she was able to finish her Ph.D. nearby. That one decision allowed her to enter the workforce as a researcher, so that Tom did not have to be the sole provider, and it gave the kids access to a wonderful city. As a result, their low-cost lifestyle allowed them the flexibility to live in Washington, D.C., for a year while she accepted a fellowship at the National Institutes of Health. Tom was able to shut down his law office for a year and join her.

Margaret says one of her biggest lifestyle influences was her father, an editor at the *Des Moines Register,* her hometown paper. She observed that for her father, by the time he was sixty, work seemed to be "an intrusion on an otherwise pleasant life. He was involved in elder hostels and community theater. He would've retired earlier if he could."

As it stands now, she thinks she won't be working much beyond seventy, but that's fine with her. She's only begun to share her knowledge and wisdom on aging and relationships with a population that sorely needs some insights to guide them. Margaret's journey is an example of not wanting to leave a livelihood too soon, and for her there's no implicit reason to leave her job any earlier than she has to. You may find yourself in a similar situation, and that's okay, because you may feel you're contributing more in your occupation than you would outside of it. While early retirement is a great idea for some, you can still obtain a new prosperity and not radically change your work and life. Margaret's quite honest about her love of her work: "Leaving the workforce [early] has never appealed to me. I can do what I want to do now within the context of my work and life." Nevertheless she has some solid advice for early retirees. It's nearly impossible to summarize her marvelous work, but here are a few key points:

- Once you get beyond the three P's—passion, procreation, and production—you still need life skills to get you through the next phases of your life. That includes further developing credibility, honor, and likability.

- When it comes to the relationship with your significant other, growth is critical for both of you. You need to ask yourself, is your partner interested in growing? The worst situation is where one partner is growing and the other isn't interested.

- You need to look at your options and know what you're good at. Look back at your working career. What did you like to do?

- With your children, you will probably prefer intimacy at a distance, the feeling that they are doing okay but not with you. Are you still willing to invest in them as persons?

- Your life beyond work also comes down to vitalization. What makes you feel most alive? What gives you pleasure?

There's Nothing Wrong with Working Part-Time or Reentering the Job Market

What if you discover that golf, tennis, volunteerism, and traveling isn't enough for you? What if you find out, after some downtime, that you need some good old-fashioned labor in your life? Would you consider yourself a failure if you reentered the workforce? A new prosperity is not a black-and-white reality. It's a flexible perception of what you need to do to maintain a healthy personal ecology. In order to program yourself for continuing prosperity, you need to manage the transition from full-time work to a different schedule. Viewing a number of different work-retirement transition options will help you adjust to the change—or allow you to change your decision at a later date after trying out a reduced work schedule.

Some people need that daily routine of going to the office or *any* workplace, for that matter. Here are some new prosperity models for you to review for your post-retirement reality:

You gradually leave work by phasing down your hours. It's a transition plan that lets you ease out of the full-time routine—or decide you don't want a part-time job at all. If your employer grants you the flexibility, this is a sound option that opens the door to reduce or take on more hours, if you decide that's what you want.

You take the formal retirement, but still work as a part-time employee. My former executive editor Elliott McCleary followed this option when he turned seventy-one and still writes a column and helps out here and there. He has plenty of time to travel and to visit his children and grandchildren, and we still get to see him every week. When you work one part-time job, you are free to seek another and see how the lighter workload suits you.

You may want to volunteer at a number of activities, but take on one task for money. For example, you could do some consulting a few days or weeks a year to either bridge an income gap or "keep your hand in" in the workplace. This is essential in several professional/technical fields, where the part-time work allows you to keep up with industry developments in case you decide to return to your industry and want to stay current with changes within your line of work.

Seek a new career. You many want to work part-time so that you can go to school full-time to earn a degree, go to trade school, or earn a technical competency certificate. I was working at something else all the time I was working on my two degrees. Your new prosperity plan may be geared so that your part-time job is subsidizing your education.

Keep on working if you're not ready. Like Dr. Huyck, you may not be at the tipping point where you take the plunge and leave your livelihood altogether. Working through later years is fine—especially if you need to build up your new prosperity portfolio. If your workload is lighter at this point in your career, you can start increasing the hours you spend at your nonwork activities, so the transition isn't such a dramatic exit from one kind of work to another. You won't be alone. The American Association of Retired Persons estimates that 58 million over age forty-five will be in the workforce by 2006—some 40 percent of the total working population. Besides, it's not unusual to be able to retire early but still *want* to work (see below).

EARLY RETIREES STILL WANT TO WORK

No. of Extra Working Years Desired	Men (55–64)	Women (50–59)
1 to 2	12%	20%
3 to 5	43%	41%
6 or more	45%	39%

Source: Commonwealth Fund

Reviewing and Restoring Relationships

There is little doubt that you'll have time for a lot of activities and different types of work under your new prosperity plan. You'll also have plenty of time to explore relationships: between you and your spouse/significant other, siblings, children, friends, relatives, community, workplaces. And then there's the personal ecology between you and your health, well-being, wealth, and spiritual persona. Planning a list of activities is fairly simple, but to have a complete program for prosperity, you'll need to examine relationships. The following are a few key suggestions from Dr. Huyck:

- **Health:** "Appropriate dietary regimes and regular exercise will defer the inevitable effects of aging, although one must work more and more rigorously to bring about the same effects."

- **Wealth:** "Job opportunities are mostly yours to discover; few traditional employment counselors will know what to do with your skills and expertise or how to translate your experience into terms employers understand. You can always start your own business. Lots of people recognize a market for a specialized product or skills—and offer it for a price."

- **Have a love affair . . .** "with your spouse or someone else. Both men and women come to appreciate the more diverse, nonverbal qualities of sensuality, which become preeminent in the later years."

- **Divorce . . .** "your spouse, and/or your children. If the relationship has become intolerable, consider the alternatives."

- **Make a new friend, younger than you are.** "Reach out to someone different, whose life experience is different from yours, and who has a different perspective on how things are and should be."

- **Make a new friend, older than you are.** "Many old people are alone, and would love to have someone come along and take an interest in them and give them a necessary assist."

- **Learn something new.** "As long as it is novel enough to stretch your brain, to create synapses in your brain cortex, and make you feel alive again."

- **Pass on what you know.** "Join or create a learning exchange, where you can share what you know and trade with someone who knows something you don't know."

- **Preserve what you cherish.** "Organize and document the family pictures and history, work as a guide/historian at the local history museum, preserve the church archive, found a local history museum and get together exhibits that illustrate the important people and precedents."

- **Agitate for what you believe in.** "Write letters to your congressmen, senators, and newspapers. Whatever you find offensive, shocking, dismaying, let someone know."

- **Be a benefactor.** "Carefully select some fledgling group that is struggling to do something you believe in, enjoy, or care about. Take all the funds you've been distributing to various worthwhile organizations and put them all into this group." This action also extends to protecting parks, organizing social issue groups and athletic teams.

- **Explore internal space.** "Such explorations can be fascinating and liberating." Keep a journal.

- **Laugh and live it up in your own way.** "Devise your own strategies. Why not?"

Revisiting Your Failures

I'm not quite sure why, but this is the part of crafting a new prosperity that I liked the most after I reviewed it. It makes me chuckle every time I do it. Without a doubt, to build a decent and sustainable new prosperity, you need to revisit your failures. Part of success in life isn't having one string of victories after another, it's failing repeatedly—and learning from your mistakes. Failure builds us up, gives us insight, and metamorphoses knowledge into wisdom the way a caterpillar becomes a butterfly. It's like Thomas Edison and his struggle to invent the lightbulb after a thousand variations in filament. By eliminating the materials that would burn out, he narrowed down to the perfect choice that would blaze on and bring electric light to the world. If you visit his labs, you see he surrounded himself with his failures, then took a nap on a little couch in the corner when he got tired. Genius in life is sometimes looking at where you've been and knowing when to take a nap and try again when you wake up.

If we're truly honest with ourselves, most of us have a pretty long list of failures and we should take time to write them down. This exercise, however, isn't designed to demean, it's designed to enrich and liberate. When you put your failure list in a drawer and reread it a week or a month later, you'll laugh. Maybe you'll cry. This is *not* the grand total of your life, however. And it's certainly not an exercise in humiliation. Building a new prosperity requires a new *perspective*. Most of the events we pencil into our lives are not failures, they are triumphs of learning and experience. For everything you thought you really bungled, hopefully you walked away with an insight. Maybe you weren't meant to be that Olympic figure skater or that hot-shot corporate attorney or that prize-winning artist. The fact is, you did these things because they made you feel alive at times when you needed to do them. That doesn't mean you can't fine-tune some of them or revisit them as passionate pursuits. And nobody' s expecting you to settle old scores. The fact is nobody's really watching now as you revisit old passions. You don't have to succeed at them. You've already made a choice of livelihood. You don't have to make a penny from your pursuits, but if you do, then *"Sto lat"* (a Polish toast meaning "May you live a hundred years").

The only thing linear about life is that we move from birth to death. Everything else in between is like an ant trail; we try to move our little caravan around major obstacles and it's a squiggly path with lots of switchbacks. So let's do some *failurizing*. Keep in mind that a broad definition of failure is something you haven't succeeded at in some point of your life. These are not devastating life events such as burning down your house because you failed to realize that smoking in bed is a bad idea. These are activities and turns of events that were less than fulfilling in some aching way. You want to examine unrealized goals that give you pause when you review your life. Of course, review things you were good at but never really took to the pinnacle of your powers. You now have a lot more experience, education, and wisdom behind you.

Some of the items on my list below are things I knew I would hate or were opportunities I never pursued. For example, there was one time I felt I was failing at journalism (and I still do on occasion), so I applied to the Central Intelligence Agency. When the first interview broached the question "Have you ever smoked marijuana and who were you smoking it with," I knew I would be a failure as a spook. Other items are less subtle. I've played a lot of musical instruments, but consider myself failures at them because of my ambivalence toward them. So there was a love-hate relationship that didn't translate into success that applies to a lot of things we do.

When you're done with the list, throw it in a drawer or file and review it later. Then cross-reference it with your "passions" list from step 5. You may find some things you want to pursue the rest of your life. I'll go first and give you my list to give you some ideas:

THE AUTHOR'S NOMINAL FAILURES

Activity	What Happened	What I Do Now
Track & Field	Tore Achilles tendon	Walk a lot
Basketball	Wasn't too coordinated	Play as much as possible
Gymnastics	No upper-body strength	50 push-ups a day
Entering U of Chicago	Poor math scores	Teach part-time there, use statistics in work
Violinist	Didn't like practice	Play infrequently
Pianist	Didn't like practice	Playing more and more, lessons
French Horn	Learned it to join h.s. band	Don't play, don't miss it
Guitar	Picked it up during college	Play from time to time
Wedding Musician	Did it for $ in college	Don't miss it

Activity	What Happened	What I Do Now
Newspaper Publisher	Didn't make enough $	Too much work, prefer writing
Book Publisher	Broke even	Might try it again
Pre-med Student	Didn't want to study hard	Right decision
Psychologist	Got B.A. in psych	May revisit, I'm no scientist
Civil Servant	Aced exam for G job	Didn't want to do it, okay by me
Career Military	Could've gone to Academy	Right decision, I'm a pacifist
CIA	Did one interview	A really good decision
Drawing	Doodled mostly	Try it again
Photography	Getting there	Bought a good camera
Public Relations	Tried it, didn't do well	Still learning
Naturalist	Always a passion	Ongoing
Teacher	Started recently	Love it, will do more
Speaker	Always loved	Will do much more
Fisherman	Tried it many times	Ambivalence, seasickness
Traveler	Always loved	Will do more of it with family

Activity	What Happened	What I Do Now
Writer	Lifelong pursuit	Still working at it
Journalist	Livelihood	May do less, but still love it
Poet	A passion	Will do more
Volunteer	Started in last 2 yrs.	Love it, will do more
Remodeler	Just finished house	Ten years is enough, we're moving
Investor	Learned as adult	Will do more

Now you do your list. The reason I've stuck this exercise in near the end of this book is because it's pretty heavy self-analysis. Sort of like doing your taxes: nobody feels good about the thought of it at first, but when you're finished, you feel this immense sense of relief and reward. Some things you tried worked out. You made some decent decisions and some bad decisions. Your bad decisions didn't kill you. You have a destiny and you may be able to see it in your failures—and progress to wisdom. This is your life, but it's not over yet.

"We all have a particular life to live with particular difficulties and joys to experience," writes Harry Moody in his classic *The Five Stages of the Soul* (Doubleday, 1997). "We are given this life not through accident or bad luck or good luck, but through the ineluctable destiny that belongs to each of us and that in some vastly mysterious way we have chosen for ourselves. We cannot escape from our destiny, but must say yes to it, down to the last detail."

I don't believe you can chart yourself a new prosperity unless you look your failures square in the eye and pick a handful of things you know your life wouldn't be complete without having at least tried them without reservation. The key now is that you don't have to see them as "time-wasters that don't bring in any money." You're free to see them for what they are—an integral part of your personal ecology. You need to understand your relationship to them before you go on.

You can have all the money in the world to retire on, but prosperity comes when you've balanced your personal ecology and put your money to use for self-development. Anybody can figure out a spending portrait and pay the bills. Anybody can get on a plane to any part of the planet. To find *yourself,* you need this road map of your past. That's where the journey begins. This is an active pursuit, however. Prosperity can end quickly if you become a couch potato with the TV remote in your hand. You probably won't be able to maintain your health in that situation and your mind will go south fast. The most beautiful account I know that describes the malady of choosing riches at the expense of personal ecology comes from Izaak Walton in *The Compleat Angler:*

> We see but the outside of the rich man's happiness: few consider him to be like the silkworm, that, when she seems to play, is, at the same time, spinning her own bowels, and consuming herself. And this is what rich men do; loading themselves with corroding cares, to keep what they have, probably unconscionably, got. Let us, therefore be thankful for health and a competence, and above all, for a quiet conscience.

Are you a "silkworm"? Are you picking out your competencies and pursuing them with passion in your new prosperity? Or are you going to be afraid of yourself and be consumed by "corroding cares"?

The New Prosperity Continuum: Moving Forward

To program yourself for a balanced new prosperity, you need a sense of self and to determine what kind of life you want. If you don't have a clue, here are some suggestions:

Talk to others who've retired early. What are they doing with their time? Are they working at anything new?

Plan out a typical week. What will you be doing to fill the void of not going to work? What will you be working at in terms of labor, soul-work, play-work, and other newly defined types of work? Make a list of things you want to do.

Make small plans and purchases. Don't take that trip around the world in the first two years. Try a year without buying the big boat, a new car, or second home. See what basic living feels like and how far your money goes.

A Philosophy of Retirement: What's Yours?

Since you're considering a whole new way of regarding work, leisure, and the rest of your life, you'll need a guiding philosophy to get you through those frozen moments of doubt. Below is a table showing a side-by-side comparison of new prosperity with the old retirement model. You may conclude that the old model is best, and that's okay. If the column on the left agrees with you, then read on, we'll explore some more ideas on how to program your new prosperity for the rest of your life. If the column on the right is where you're at, you're going to be late for your tee time. See how early retirement feels and what's missing. Fill in the gaps. Better yet, see what kind of retirement fits you best by checking off what applies to you:

NEW PROSPERITY VERSUS TRADITIONAL RETIREMENT: YOU CHOOSE

New Prosperity Values	Old Retirement Values
Seeking balance through personal ecology	Leaving workforce cold turkey
Continuous education/ reeducation	I know too much already
Continuous spiritual/ emotional growth	I've been to church

New Prosperity Values	Old Retirement Values
Reentering, restoring community	I'm getting out of this neighborhood
Investments still growing and working	Fixed-income lifestyle
A reemergence into life	A retreat from life
Chance to pursue passions	Chance to play golf all the time
Dynamic model—change is needed	Static model—I'll stay the same
Part of a global community	Member of gated community
Transition to new life	Don't bother me
New definitions of work	Total work avoidance
Intellectual challenges	I'm not paid to think anymore
A quest every day	Every day is a vacation
Do it now	Maybe tomorrow

Spirituality, Religion, and Callings

You won't suddenly need to go out and "find religion," because it's unlikely that you'll swallow a lot of dogma at this point in your life anyway. If you have been practicing a religion—or choose to adopt one—you'll have more time to explore it, especially in a volunteer/ service role. Huston Smith, the renowned religious historian, notes that in Judaism whenever you do a good deed, or mitzvah, a new angel is created. "Whatever else happens to one's soul, that angel is still there working on behalf of humanity. It's the noblest view of angels I know of."

At the very least, you can find a happy medium between the spirit in yourself, others, places, and ideas when you have more time to pursue it. Or even adopt a life of *ora et laborum,* a life of prayer and work, that helps balance your many lives. Meditation or meditative bodywork (like yoga, tai chi, qigong, and other Eastern disciplines) is also something you can explore. Spirituality is a general approach to this awareness of the infinite energy of the universe working through all people and things. You can have spirituality without religion but not vice versa. You can't have either without a sound personal ecology that's based on a universal well-being, or as the Dalai Lama said, "All religions carry the message of love, compassion, sense of brotherhood, sisterhood, and tolerance."

Most true religions capture our hearts and imagination and allow us to grow spiritually. Although we may not formally attend religious services, phenomena like miracles—which more than 126 million Americans have told the U. S. Census Bureau they believe in—are part of a life of faith and spirit. We may identify this universal force with angels or the Holy Spirit. A precursor to this higher awareness is *mindfulness,* an omnipresent awareness of the unseen powers of life. Thich Nhat Hanh, a Vietnamese Buddhist monk, remarks that "mindfulness is very much like the Holy Spirit. Both are agents of healing. When you have mindfulness, you have love and understanding, you see more deeply, and you can heal the wounds in your own mind."

In regard to healing, faith has been known to play a strong part in helping us live longer. Religion involves social connectedness, a link between people that often helps us to maintain a healthy mental attitude. And studies show that those who rate low in social connectedness "are two to four times more likely to die [earlier] than those who rate high."

Surveys have also shown that regular "attenders" of a particular religion live longer and healthier lives. Frequent attenders, on average, died at age eighty-three; those who never went to services died at seventy-five. According to the National Health Interview Survey, that "faith factor" translated to a 10 percent lower mortality rate for men and 34 percent lower rate for women. That doesn't mean that if you regularly practice the religion of your choice you are guaranteed to live longer, because there are hundreds of other factors involved in longevity. The basic insight here is that religion may act as a stress reliever and way of coping with life's many traumas.

"Religion offers powerful ways to cope with major life stresses, particularly health problems and experience of loss," notes Dr. Harold Koenig of the Center for Study of Religion, Spirituality, and Health in Durham, North Carolina. It's not necessarily true that going to services every day will add more days to your life. It's possible, however, that a greater spiritual awareness reduces the stress of constant interpersonal conflict (as you may have experienced in the workplace). Rolling Thunder, a Native American (Cherokee Paint) activist and philosopher, asserted before he died in 1997, "Anyone can be a spiritual person by maintaining internal harmony and compassion [personal ecology]. When you maintain internal harmony and compassion, the answers would come to you, you would know what to do to cope with problems and how to apply yourselves to make life better for others."

The universal awareness that religion and spirituality bring may also bring you to a *calling*, a vocation that urges you from within. We discern this calling by knowing what it is not: It's not a hobby, craft, interest, pursuit, or study. Callings involve pure faith, a sense of urgency that will not allow us to do anything else in life until we heed the call. "In saying yes to our calls, we bring flesh to word and form to faith," finds Greg Levoy, author of *Callings* (Harmony, 1997).

A calling may include anything from becoming a minister in your church to helping homeless people to building a park. It is a deep commitment that you abide by, in contrast to an apprenticeship merely to learn something. Beethoven heard the call to create great symphonies. Van Gogh was called to painting. Mother Teresa was called to help the poor in Calcutta. Although I'm not in this league, I feel called to meet people and tell their stories. Here's a brief comparison of two related concepts that may help you:

APPRENTICESHIP VS. CALLINGS

Apprenticeship is . . .	Calling is . . .
Pursued	Chosen
Planned	Sought
Labor-work	Soul-work

Apprenticeship is . . .	Calling is . . .
Structured	Unstructured
Learning by doing	Learning through inner experience
Something we adapt to	Something that changes us
Deductive	Intuitive
Didactic	Revealing
Satisfying	Challenging
Instructive	Transforming

Charity

If you have achieved the ability to take an early retirement, you may want to share your prosperity with others. That doesn't mean cutting a check to every needy charitable organization on your list, however. You can devote your time and talents to worthy causes, as Dr. Huyck suggested earlier in this chapter. You may offer *diakonia*, or a spiritual service through a religious group or organization. Or consider a tithe, where 10 percent of your income goes to helping others. Muslims suggest you donate 2.5 percent of your assets, which they call *zakat*, which may be donated to the impoverished, unemployed, or needy individuals. How much you choose to give, though, is entirely up to you. Money is something we all want to have our hands on all the time, yet few of us understand how money touches us and others.

Your charity is part of a personal ecology that balances out your wealth with the many needs of your community. Talmudic scholars suggest that good fortune should be complemented with creating abundance around you, or practicing *tzedakah,* which translated by Rabbi Nilton Bonder means "the

> **NEW PROSPERITY TIP**
>
> Some charities need your help more than others. Adopt a charity by employing your best skills to help them. Draw up a list of groups you will support in other ways or by making contributions.

art of justicing." That means helping society with the money you have and using this resource to alleviate inequalities in an economic culture.

On the whole, your new prosperity embraces a moral dimension that you may not have considered. Probing the reality that "I don't have to work at something I don't like the rest of my life" involves recognition that you've been given a gift. Your insights will benefit you in your new prosperity and provide guidance for others. Heed the advice of the monk Thomas Merton, who said, "the success or failure of a man's [or woman's] spiritual life depends on the clarity with which he is able to see and judge the motives of his moral acts."

We need a lens through which to see our own actions. That's why listing your failures in the exercise in this chapter is so important. As an early retiree, you'll need a clear perspective on moral issues as well as financial ones.

Finding Sacred Things and Places

There are certain places and things we visit that are so spiritually powerful that our life is an empty vessel without them. In my own experience, I've found any number of places to be sacred because I've felt the power from them. Those places include: my own church (Transfiguration, in Wauconda, Illinois), Canterbury Cathedral (England), Grace Cathedral (San Francisco), the Great Pyramid at Chichen Itza (Mexico), New York City, San Francisco, Chicago, London, Paris, Rome, St. Peter's Basilica, the Sistine Chapel, Notre Dame (Paris), Mauthausen (a concentration camp in Austria), Stonehenge, the Louvre, the Auditorium (Chicago), the Alps, the Grand Canyon, the Grand Tetons, the Blue Ridge Mountains, Lake Superior, the Big Cypress Swamp, Cape Hatteras, Avoca Prairie, the Olympic Peninsula, the Sonoran Desert, the Volo Bog, the Lake District (England), Muir Woods, and the two-hundred-year-old cottonwood tree in my former front yard. These places move me to feel that others have left their energy there and I'm benefiting from it. I think the soul is a receptacle of energy and that sacred places are storehouses of this vital force.

Do you have any ideas now of the sacred places and things in your life? Maybe you haven't been there yet. There is a spirit of place wherever there are living things—even Death Valley is brimming with life if you know where to look. I've always considered our front and back yards to be sacred places, and even certain apartments (roaches and all). Look at the trees, the grass, and the flowers or the snow in winter (if you are so blessed). This is our space, our retreat from the world. If this isn't sacred, then no place is.

A thunderstorm was rolling in from the southwest one summer day. Kathleen had taken her horse, Tara, out for a ride with our German shepherd, Ella, at her side. As the wind picked up and the sky turned bluish brown, I became concerned and walked out into the backyard and then onto the farm field behind us to see if I could spot them. They were far on the horizon, so I was hoping they could get back before the storm hit. A midwestern thunderstorm rolls in faster than you can ever imagine. All of the fury of nature is unleashed in a few minutes before the sky turns blue or the humidity overwhelms your senses.

Kathleen had made it as far as twenty feet in front of the barn when the bony finger of Zeus came down upon us. She had just dismounted from Tara when lightning blasted a towering ancient oak tree no more than five feet away, hurling bark some forty feet. Tara spun around dazed, but for some reason the normally skittish thoroughbred didn't bolt. Tara held her ground, then later snorted proudly that she had kept her cool despite being almost incinerated by the fiery fist of heaven. Ella rubbed her sensitive ears. Sacred places are powerful places that store, condense, and release our energy and that of nature's, then liberate this force in great bursts during languid August afternoons or January snowstorms. While one place is not more sacred than another—your backyard isn't less sacred than a cathedral—you need to pick some places that will allow you to creatively employ the ebb and flow of your many life-energies. If that means relocating to a different climate, city, community, or country, experiment with it in your new prosperity.

Sacred places are essential to our humanity. We should visit them often in our travels to remind us of the blessings of prosperity and what enduring things prosperity has given us, whether from the hand of man or the hand of God. So, make a list:

SACRED PLACES IN MY LIFE

1.

2.

3.

4.

5.

6.

7.

8.

9.

10.

It's All About Balancing

Can you have *too much* spirituality, religion, and relationships in your life as you move forward? Certainly. That's why it's important to realize that personal ecology is all about balancing. What makes it work is a *combination* of different pursuits, activities, relationships with others, and the eternal presence.

One summer my big brother Steve decided he wanted to replace the engine on an old Chevy truck he bought. He wanted to drop in a hot V-8 that his boss, a rust-proofing contractor, had given him. Since this was a time before computer-controlled timing and pollution-control devices, it was, on the surface, a relatively simple matter. He had just trained in mechanical repair (and was on his way to earning an associate's degree in it), so this was the acid test: dropping in a new engine and making it hum. He spent hours preparing, removing bolts and belts and placing parts in piles where he could later identify and replace them. He pulled the old engine out with relative ease. The new engine popped in fairly simply, but after hours and hours of tinkering, swearing, and sweating—it was the middle of summer—it wouldn't turn over. He couldn't hear what was wrong, because he has been deaf from birth, so he had to *feel* what it was and think hard. He had all the tools, he had all the parts. One small thing knocked it out of balance. Days went by and he tried everything he knew. Finally, *hrrrrrm, hrrrrrm,* the growl of nearly 400-plus cubic inches of steel pulsating like a panther ready to pounce. It was a triumph that taught him you can't overlook even the smallest details when restarting your engine. He's not sure to this day what prevented the engine from running, but surmises it could've been a single bolt. When one element is missing, the whole unit fails.

It's all about personal ecology; the parts add up to the whole. The whole simply can't work without all of its whole parts, or *holons,* which are the separate components of your spirit, your work, your financial life, and your community at large.

Where You've Been, Where You're Going

1. Focus on the transition to early retirement. Do you want to phase down your hours, work part-time, start a new career, or just work a while longer?

2. Revisit your failures. Are there areas you want to reexplore?

3. Reexamine your many relationships and explore ways of improving them.

4. Religion and spirituality call us further into the mystery of life. Reserve a big space for them in your new prosperity plan. Find or visit sacred things and places.

Putting It All Together and Launching Your Personal Pursuit of Happiness

In the midst of the turmoil of too-rapid change, an extraordinary light has arisen. Factors unique in history are poised to help us become more than we thought we could ever be.
— Jean Houston, *A Passion for the Possible*

When Frank Butler took the golden parachute offered him when he was fifty-eight, he did not have a clear idea of what he was going to do when he walked out of his office for the last time. He wanted to go to a developing country with the Peace Corps or Vista or as a missionary. As a former CEO of an Eastman Kodak division, he was following his heart to help others, although most men of his station choose the life of leisure.

It wasn't that Frank was in a hurry to leave his job, his company, or his country. He enjoyed the challenges of his career and led a unit that produces gelatins, which are the heart of every photographic film product (silver halide). The challenges and power of his position compelled him to pass up two earlier buyout packages in the 1980s. You rarely hear workers leaving a company say anything like what he said about Kodak: "It was an industrial utopia. We had all the advantages of a small plant but had the solid backing of a strong international corporation."

Life outside Kodak was rich and fulfilling as well for Frank. He served on fifteen boards of directors for various nonprofit organizations. They all wanted his management acumen, his ability to motivate people to do difficult things on a daily basis. When the third buyout package came around, he remembers committing several hours to prayer and meditation, hoping to hear an answer "that wells up from within." He had been all over the world to see poverty firsthand and felt a personal mission to do something about it in his own society, a "culture that's incredibly wealthy but tends to isolate us from the harsh realities."

He worked with the Sisters of Charity to found the fledgling Ministry of Money to show affluent people like himself that they can perform work in a developing country then return to teach and live more modest and reflective lifestyles in the United States. It's what he calls "getting out of your normal culture to crack your shell." It's his mission.

"I felt called to the business world, though. As I prospered, I realized I had a job that was the dream of most people." So he went to India and met Mother Teresa.

"She asked me why I was in Calcutta, so I told her about my retirement plans and doing a mission overseas. She put her hand on my knee and looked me in the eye and said, 'Don't do that. Go back and work in America, where God has put you.' It was like the word of God."

Since his meeting with Mother Teresa, Frank's gained some insights into how people live here—observations that you rarely hear on the evening news or during Sunday football games. Instead of serving the poor overseas, Frank's helping the affluent in this country to understand the poverty and need that is within their communities. The philosophy of his Ministry of Money is that "a soup kitchen for some at home can be as meaningful and growth-evoking in compassion and justice as going to Kosovo," to quote

Jim Wallis in *Call to Conversion* (Harper & Row, 1981). Frank sees himself as a peacemaker in "reverse missions" that are attempting to bring into balance the profound abundance of the United States with the poverty of others at home and abroad. This is not a typical point of view of most ex-CEOs, but one anchored in sound personal ecology that focuses on the relationship between spirit and wealth. Not only is his ministry giving him a centered life in his retirement, but it's helping others to examine their worldviews.

"I've never seen such loneliness in the poverty of affluence. God does change hearts. We know our lives have impact. My son Peter died when he was forty after a ten-year battle with cancer. At the funeral, his boss said how much they would miss him and that whenever they had a 'people problem,' they would consult him. . . . Pouring out your life for others is how we find deep joy."

Frank is ever active in living a life that touches others. His wisdom can't be distilled, but here are a few of his ideas to reflect upon:

- When you are faced with a difficult decision, consult with those you respect, then make the decision in spite of them.

- The most effective form of leadership is serving. As a CEO, Frank learned that he could employ his values in the workplace.

- There is no one formula for spiritual guidance after you leave the workforce. "God made us unique and meant for us to share our stories, not make prescriptions for anyone else."

- We're called to give to charity. Frank believes in—and practices—tithing where 10 percent of his annual income goes to charity. But we give as much as we're able to contribute.

- For sounding boards, join a small, intimate support group. Go on retreats. Attend seminars.

A New Identity and Relationship with Money

Frank Butler's mission is a noble one. But trying to teach those steeped in wealth the virtues of simple charity and sharing has to be one of the toughest jobs on the planet. After all, we live in our own little gated communities behind large walls of money. Our own prosperity is often a barrier to the pain, poverty, and social problems around us. Although my personal ecology revolves around how I relate to the least fortunate around me, I am by no means suggesting that you adopt this worldview, but it certainly would enrich your life in untold ways. A mutual fund can make you rich over time, but only a giving heart can enrich others.

What is your relationship to your money? Do you realize that if you have a balanced relationship to it, you'll diminish a lot of inner turmoil? Money is responsible for a host of conflicts in our lives from overspending to not spending enough on ourselves. Putting money in a spiritual perspective allows you to transcend the idea of whether you have "enough." George Kinder, a financial planner friend who has penned the insightful *Seven Stages of Money Maturity* (Delacorte, 1999), writes, "Money is a critical link between the interior and exterior. If we have a poor relationship with money, it is likely we also have a poor relationship with our inner beings."

To know our inner identity, we must first acknowledge that what Western culture insists is our "consumer identity" is false and misleading. Although we can gain some insights from what we buy and how we spend, those are illusions that represent miniscule parts of our personality. A 21-foot cabin cruiser is not who we are. A designer label doesn't tell the world our inner longings. A pair of running shoes won't expose our soul to anyone. These consumer society–driven goods are merely symbols of our money identity, although they say nothing about our relationship to it. These goods are only signs of how we spent it. "It isn't money that runs our economy, but vanity," observed Philip Slater in his classic cultural critique, *The Pursuit of Loneliness* (Beacon, 1970). It's easy to show our vanity in what we wear, drive, or live in. Not so simple to bare our souls, which is fundamental to a new prosperity.

Affluence may be corrupting after a certain point—it makes you lose perspective on how most of the world lives. And if you can work at anything you want now, you may forget that your *identity* is still a work in progress. Surveys show that despite widespread prosperity in the West, we are no happier than we were forty years ago. Paul Wachtel in *The Poverty of Affluence* (New Society, 1989) observes, "One might well expect improvements in the material basis of life to be strongly associated with improvements in feelings of well-being. But the middle class in the United States, Western Europe, and other industrialized nations constitutes what one might call an 'asymptote culture,' a culture in which the contribution of material goods to life satisfaction has reached a point of diminishing returns."

Yet how do sustain our new prosperity? When and if that lump sum stares us in the face, there will be incredible temptation to buy the best car, boat, or vacation home we can find. The advertising all around us implores us to give in and take the plunge in 10,000 different ways. There's advertising in the schools, in parks, and on people's bodies. How do we tune out the billions of messages that pollute our minds with manufactured identities? As Thomas Berry, author of *The Dream of the Earth* (Sierra Club, 1988), opines about advertising, "Its presence has become so all-pervasive that the populace is surrounded on all sides with appeals to buy and consume, appeals so urgent, so competitive, that they begin to take on hysterical dimensions." Anyone who watches TV infomercials knows exactly what Berry is talking about. We have to draw the line somewhere, especially if we want to obtain—and maintain—a new prosperity. And "simplifying" our lives by cleaning out our closets doesn't make the relentless howl of advertising go away.

Thomas Moore suggests in *Care of the Soul* (HarperCollins, 1992) that we need to separate the wheat from the chaff when it comes to our relationship with money. "We have to distinguish between shadow qualities of money [promoted in advertising] that are part of its soulfulness and symptoms of money gone berserk." We also need to cease fusing our personal identity with that as consumers. After all, as Joe Dominguez and Vicki Robin, the authors of the splendid *Your Money or Your Life* (Penguin, 1992), assert, "According to the dictionary, to *consume* is to 'destroy, to squander, to use up.'" Mark Burch in *Simplicity* (New Society, 1995) adds, "A consumptive society is neither materialistic nor spiritual. It enjoys less and less and tries to consume more and more."

It's possible to overcome the bombardment of spending messages we take in every day. The key to sustaining new prosperity in the face of this assault is to maintain balance between our inner identity—who we really are—and our money, possessions, family, and community. "People are not only aware of what will bring their lives more into balance, but many people are actively making changes in their lives to bring this about," find Joel and Michelle Levey in *Living in Balance* (Conari, 1998). In the context of a sound personal ecology, you can achieve balance by:

- **Learning.** Explore what you don't know and what you want to understand. Create what Willis Harman, former president of the Institute of Noetic Sciences, called "a learning society," where "the occupational focus of most people is learning and developing in the broadest sense."

- **Reduce the wastefulness in your life.** What does it take to make you happy? Is there anything you can live without? Give it to charity. Avoid what social critic Vance Packard called "the waste makers," those companies that produce things that most people throw away. Cleaning out your closet, basement, and garage won't clean up the excesses in your life, but it's a symbolic start to a new prosperity. You can respect yourself, help the planet, and keep your life simple by cutting out the physical goods that cause clutter and waste.

- **Since your need for work will not end, connect the work you do with your identity.** Avoid what social historian Carolyn Merchant calls "the psychological alienation caused by a person's daily labor for wages in a business or industry owned by another individual [or stockholders] who reaps both money and a higher standard of living as a result." You are leaving the conventional workforce for a reason. Your loss of identity needn't continue in your new prosperity. (Read steps 5 and 9 again if you need to.)

- **Do something that "makes you unequivocably and totally happy."** Michael Fogler suggests this in *Un-Jobbing: The Adult*

Liberation Handbook (Free Choice, 1997). If there's at least one passionate pursuit you identified in step 5, make it the cornerstone of your new prosperity.

- **Forget about the status of spending or showing how much money you have.** That leads to unbridled wastefulness anyway. Status-seeking may cloak certain insecurities about our identity. Andrew Hacker, in *Money* (Touchstone, 1997), hit it on the head when he observed, "The history of our time has created for Americans a culture based on status and style, seduction and temptation, and symbols of success used to mask the anxieties of uncertain identities."

- **Concentrate on your *self*, not your self-image, that illusion we present to the world.** We are so much more complicated than advertisers would have us believe. Review your failures, take on projects, indulge in life's many events. Stop comparing yourself to others and "comparing our own lifestyle and possessions to those of a select group of people we respect and want to be like," as Julie Schor reflects in *The Overspent American* (Basic Books, 1998).

- **What has meaning to you has infinite value.** The search for meaning can be your quest now, and you can abandon the idea that *more* (of anything, particularly money) is what you need. If you've ever been addicted to money and its many garish faces, then now's a time to enter a twelve-step program. Moreover, as Barbara Brandt reveals in *Whole Life Economics* (New Society, 1995), "Money addiction means that people measure their worth by how much money they have; the lives of people with less money are less valued, and people without moneymaking opportunities learn to devalue themselves." When you are freed from your need to make money the old-fashioned way—by slaving for it—what will you do? Write down some goals. Anything that you want to do now. Then craft a plan of action. That's the next step.

DREAM GOALS

Goal	How Will I Pursue It?
1.	
2.	
3.	
4.	
5.	

Happiness and Prosperity

Can you believe I tortured you all this time with jeremiads on spending, investing, and passionate pursuits and didn't mention the most important thing? A new prosperity is about the *pursuit* of happiness. Although ascetics throughout the ages have probably been quite happy without money, they didn't need to buy health insurance, pay property taxes, or worry about the global economy. But you've figured all of that out by now, so here are some more insights into happiness, money, and your new prosperity.

Don't Worry, Be Prosperous

1. If you can save more than you make, make sure to invest in yourself, your family, and your community by sharing your wealth.

2. What you don't need, give away. You can donate clothes, cars, computers, and just about anything to a charity that needs it.

3. Walk around, notice things. Does your community need you in a way that only you can help? Ask questions. Get mad. Do something. Part of prosperity is getting emotionally involved in a shared prosperity.

4. Take some time to talk to yourself about things. There's nothing wrong with talking to—and with—yourself. You might even get an intelligent response.

5. Life is full of jagged edges and it's important to cut yourself now and again. We all bleed. We can heal quickly if we see our failures and let them fertilize our successes.

6. There is no big picture, only a lot of snapshots. Your life is a series of portraits and group shots. Who's smiling now?

7. Be a fervent "social capitalist." Find ways of sharing your knowledge about anything with those who need it. That's the best way of investing in the future of society and leaving a legacy.

8. Listen and be quiet for a while. Life speaks to us in the moment between heartbeats and tears.

9. You're getting older and more aware of what it takes to give you pleasure, joy, exhilaration, and bliss. Follow whatever course of spirituality and religion you need to obtain that perennial wisdom that connects you with the ecology of every other person and thing.

10. Ignore all of the aforementioned advice. Just do what you need to do, do it now and find joy in your life every day and learn to share it with others.

Be Prepared for Change, Synchronicity— Anything Can Happen

Your early retirement and new prosperity will be full of challenges, adventures, torment, grief, and joy. Most of all, it will present the prospect of change, which is difficult for most people. If you can indulge in your passionate pursuits, educate yourself in a number of areas, or just need to be a caregiver for someone else, it will profoundly change you. Sometimes opportunities and crises will appear out of nowhere, and if you are open to possibilities, then you can probably bob up like a buoy if you are prepared.

A few years ago, in pursuit of a story on funeral fraud, I had a chance to talk with Jessica Mitford, whose *American Way of Death* (Simon & Schuster, 1960) remains the classic on the subject. Ironically, despite her many witty and razor-sharp muckraking books on everything from birth to prison, she asked *me* for some investigative tips. I gave her a few nuggets that I was sure were of no value to one of the century's finest investigative writers. A few weeks went by and she said she was grateful for the morsels I had given her, as she was preparing an updated edition of her legendary funeral tome. She then asked how she could help *me*. Since I was struggling to get my books published at the time, had gone through seven agents, and was fighting with publishers over royalties, I blurted jokingly that I needed a good agent. She recommended her agent, but upon calling him he told me he wasn't looking for new clients. Then she recommended my present agent, Robert Shepard, who was responsible for getting contracts for my last book and this one. I never really got the chance to fully thank her, as she died a year after my award-winning piece on funerals was published (which, thankfully, did not lead to a book deal). Her kindness was an angelic intervention at the time. Had I taken her agent's no as the final answer on my literary career, I don't know what I would be doing today—probably trading commodities or pursuing a law degree. I only pray that my present and future work will be worthy of her praise, even though she's not physically here anymore.

> ### NEW PROSPERITY TIP
>
> If you are taking an early-retirement package, then avail yourself of any pre-retirement seminars your company may be offering and find out everything you can about it from your benefits department. These are often part of the package and include financial planning, vocational guidance, and other life-planning skills.

Nevertheless, the universe finds you in your time of need, and if you are open to others, then you'll connect with the eternal vitality and synchronicity (a spontaneous connection with others at the same time) that will sustain any kind of prosperity you can imagine. You will find the activities and people you need just by doing what you do with passion.

Fred's Flowers Keep on Growing; Tom's Craftsmanship Is There Every Day

We all leave something of ourselves behind whenever we leave a place. The ultimate goal of new prosperity is that by sacrificing and suffering, we obtain this balance where we are "leavers" instead of "takers," to quote Daniel Quinn's *Ishmael,* an ape's view of the human race. And it's not that we have to leave what Edison or Einstein left us. There are hundreds of small, elegant gifts that brighten our existence every day. We just need to look for them. My boyhood friend and neighbor Tom Stege didn't make it to forty, but he left behind the impeccable craftsmanship on my parents' home and many others. My late neighbor Fred Kueking's perennial flowers multiply and bloom in our front and back yards every spring, giving us the color and generosity that was his spirit. Larry Trausch, who was my sister-in-law's father, left a thriving business for my brother-in-law to run. My grandmother Blanche left a complete set of Dickens, some tables, and many gifts from all over the world. I may not ever know what she was really like, but I know I'm a kindred spirit and will sojourn through the Dickens with her and my daughter Sarah, who is an avid reader and lover of stories. My grandfather Frank left some of his drawing tools; I also got his genes for premature grayness and perhaps some other gifts I've yet to discover.

There is a legacy that is yours and yours alone. Your new prosperity is just an instrument that will aid you in discovering it—and passing it along. Whether you choose to follow your passion or just spend time on the delicate lacework of relationships in your life, you will need to let this elusive force take you by the hand, shake you a bit, and guide you to something much better and infinite.

Stepping Off on the Right Foot

1. If you haven't done your spending portrait, that should be your first priority.

2. Add up all sources of income, then adjust for any "prosperity savings" in mortgages/housing, transportation, and work-related expenses. Determine an adjusted monthly income level that you can comfortably live on.

3. If you haven't fully funded your retirement plans, do so. If your company doesn't offer a plan, set one up yourself.

3.

4. Invest for growth and ensure that your total rate of return is handily beating the rate of inflation over time.

4.

5. Invest in stock-index mutual funds or growth stocks to maximize your new prosperity portfolio returns.

5.

6. If you have passionate pursuits, identify them, develop them, and go for it. You may be living a long time past retirement. Get engaged with life on many levels.

6.

7. If you have children at home, plan carefully for their future and save money along the way.

7.

8. Make sure that you can sustain your portfolio's growth based on withdrawal rates, taxes, and returns.

8.

9. Identify and nurture your spiritual commitments. Revisit your failures. Further refine your own definitions of a new prosperity through reflection and practice.

9.

10. Enjoy the aging process; revel in your wisdom. Share with others the love you have to give. Enjoy your life as never before.

REFERENCES

PREFACE
Henry David Thoreau. *Walden* (Modern Library, 1937), p. 87. Always a companion when pursuing another life.

STEP 1
Ken Wilbur, *Sex, Ecology, Spirituality: The Spirit of Evolution* (Shambhala, 1995), p. 18. A masterpiece of modern philosophy that combines Western and Eastern worldviews.

Lori Simon, et al., "The Future of Work and Retirement Needs: Baby Boomers Express Their Views," *Generations* (Spring 1998). Timely research on the future of retirement.

Challenger, Gray and Christmas, "Layoffs: An Update," press release, 28 December 1998. This leading outplacement firm regularly tracks corporate layoffs.

Robert Reich, "Naptime Is Over," *New York Times Magazine,* 25 January 1998, p. 34. A wake-up call from the former U.S. secretary of labor.

AARP, "Baby Boomers Envision Retirement," survey on www.aarp.org, 28 May 1999. The research indicates that boomers may work well past retirement age.

"Lane's Labours Lost," *The Economist,* 17 June 1995. The decline of union representation in the workforce.

The Roge Report, April 1999. A financial planner's letter with decent commentary.

Employee Benefit Research Institute, *EBRI Retirement Confidence Survey* (1998) (Washington, D.C.) For more information, see survey results at www.ebri.org.

Richard Manning, *Grassland* (Viking, 1995), p. 141. A penetrating look at the past, present, and future of the great American grasslands.

Fritjof Capra, *The Web of Life: A New Scientific Understanding of Living Systems* (Anchor, 1996). The physicist ties together systems of thinking, ecology, chaos theory, and our connections.

David Korten, *When Corporations Rule the World* (Kumarian Press, 1995). An in-depth look at corporate power throughout the world and how it impacts our lives.

Dr. Martin Luther King Jr., quoted in Michael Rothschild's *Bionomics: Economy as Ecosystem* (Henry Holt, 1990). An interesting treatise that links economics with ecology.

Worldwatch Institute, *Vital Signs, 1999*. An array of facts and statistics on global population, environmental factors, and if things are getting better or worse from year to year.

STEP 2

Linda Stern, "Stupid Credit-Card Tricks to Avoid," Reuters News Service, 9 June 1999. An excellent personal finance columnist who writes for any level of reader.

Consumers Digest Auto Buying Guide (January–February, 1999). The annual *Consumers Digest* guide to vehicle prices, maintenance costs, and anything you would want to know about buying something with four wheels. Also see *IntelliChoice*'s annual guides on vehicle costs or www.intellichoice.com.

You can find information on credit, spending, and mortgages on many major personal finance Web sites. My favorites are www.bankrate.com and www.quicken.com. Not only will these sites give you hundreds of tips on how to reduce your debt load, you can shop for low-rate credit cards and mortgages and calculate how much you can save by avoiding costly items.

Andrew Tobias, *The Only Investment Guide You'll Ever Need* (Harvest Original, 1998). An engaging and funny guide to the basics of personal finance.

STEP 3

Thomas Berry, *The Dream of the Earth* (Sierra Club Books, 1985), p. 156. An elegant treatise on our place on the planet. You can apply it to your personal ecology as well.

Online retirement resources. It's difficult to calculate everything connected with an early-retirement scenario, especially in a book.

Superior resources can be found on the Internet, most of them free. These "calculators" will allow you to plug in retirement assets, inflation factors, and numerous other variables. Try the retirement software at www.vanguard.com, www.troweprice.com, www.strong-funds.com, www.fidelity.com, and www.quicken.com, then compare the results. Although these are commercial sites designed to lead you into buying mutual funds or software, they are great resources for getting started— and you don't have to buy anything. If you want to upgrade to a more sophisticated analysis of your retirement needs, buy the full versions of Quicken, T. Rowe Price's Retirement Analyzer, or any comprehensive retirement package.

STEP 4

Nearly every commercial financial Web site (see above) has all the basics on retirement plans. But don't forget to check with your employee benefits or personnel department first. They are required by law to provide you with information on defined-benefit and defined-contribution plans. Another good idea is to check the U.S. Department of Labor Web site, www.dol.gov, which has the complete law and explanation on benefits, health insurance extension (COBRA), retirement benefits, and many links.

Also see Twila Slesnick and John Suttle, *IRAs, 401(k)s and Other Retirement Plans: Taking Your Money Out* (Nolo, 1998), which explains retirement-plan withdrawals with great detail and clarity.

STEP 5

Tao Te Ching (Harper & Row, 1988), trans. Stephen Mitchell. An updated translation of one of the great classics of philosophy.

William Morris, *News from Nowhere and Other Writings* (Penguin, 1994, orig. pub. 1898). Morris's vision of "work-pleasure" is outlined in this utopian novella. The co-founder of the Arts and Crafts movement still has much to say about finding meaningful work and leisure. See also the seminal biography *William Morris* by Fiona McCarthy (Knopf, 1994).

E. F. Schumacher, *Small Is Beautiful: Economics as if People Mattered* (Harper Perennial, 1973), p. 58. A must-read if you are concerned about balancing your personal ecology with the needs of society and the planet.

Lewis Richmond, *Work as Spiritual Practice* (Broadway Books, 1999). A groundbreaking work by a businessman convert to Buddhism.

STEP 6

For a much broader treatment of index funds and cost savings, consult Dale Maley, *Index Mutual Funds: How to Simplify Your Financial Life and Beat the Pros* (Artephius, 1999). Also check www.vanguard.com and www.morningstar.net mutual fund resources.

I'm not ashamed to say that one of the most honest resources on investment clubs and stock picking is my *Investment Club Book* (Warner, 1995). I admit to many horrible stock-picking mistakes and don't fudge the numbers. For even more stock advice, see *The Late-Start Investor* (Holt, 1999).

For a humane, bare-bones treatment on retirement, see Ralph Warner's *Get a Life: You Don't Need a Million to Retire Well* (Nolo, 1996). It's a fun, engaging general book on the subject.

STEP 7

A consistently good source of information on saving money if you have a family is the newsletter *The Pocket Change Investor* (Good Advice Press, 800-255-0899, www.goodadvicepress.com). It's full of useful money-saving tips. The company also sells mortgage-payment software, books, and software that will help you pay off credit card debt.

Every major mutual fund Web site, personal finance magazine (see Resources in following section), and major financial Web site has extensive information on saving for college. My favorites include: www.smartmoney.com, www.kiplingers.com, and www.troweprice.com. Also use one of the search engines in the following section to find scholarships, loan programs, college information, and financial aid packages online.

Also consult Peter Finch and Delia Marshall, *How to Raise Kids Without Going Broke: The Complete Financial Guide for Parents* (Avon, 1999). A great resource.

STEP 8

Without question, the single best resource on long-term planning for your early-retirement portfolio is John Greaney's Retire Early Home Page, www.geocities.com/wallstreet/8257. He includes nearly every online calculator you need to project income and portfolio returns, links to other key Web sites, and vital information on every aspect of early retirement.

When shopping for insurance, use search engines (listed in Resources) to find online insurers and the lowest-cost quotes for the policies you need.

For information on Treasury securities, your first stop should be the U.S. Treasury Web site at www.ustreas.gov. Also, call the department's Treasury Direct Hotline at 800-943-6864.

STEP 9

Center for the Advancement of Health, "Getting Old: A Lot of It Is in Your Head," *Facts of Life/An Issue Briefing for Health Reporters,* vol. 3, no. 2. 1998. Excellent compilation on aging and health studies.

John Rowe and Robert Kahn, *Successful Aging* (Random House, 1998). A summary of the MacArthur Foundation study on lifestyle, aging, and health.

Tom Heymann, *The Unofficial U.S. Census: What the U.S. Census Doesn't Tell You* (Fawcett, 1991), p. 7. A concise summary of U.S. Census findings.

Morton Hunt, *The Compassionate Beast: What Science Is Discovering About the Humane Side of Mankind* (William Morrow, 1990). A thorough study of altruism by a top science writer.

Abul A 'la Mawdudi, *Towards Understanding Islam* (Message, 1986), p. 121. A useful introduction to the faith of more than one billion people.

Rabbi Nilton Bonder, *The Kabbalah of Money: Insights on Livelihood, Business, and All Forms of Economic Behavior* (Shambhala, 1996). Written by a Talmudic scholar, the insights on personal ecology and money are scintillating.

Thich Nhat Hanh, *Living Buddha, Living Christ* (Riverhead, 1995). A thoroughly engaging comparison of Christianity and Buddhism by a Vietnamese Buddhist monk. See his many other works for more explorations into "mindfulness."

William McGuire and R. F. C. Hull, eds., *C. G. Jung Speaking* (Princeton, 1977). Based on Dr. Jung's lectures and media interviews, this often overlooked text catches Jung at his most accessible and revealing moments.

Dr. Barrie Sanford Greiff, *Legacy: The Giving of Life's Treasures* (Regan Books, 1999). A charming and soulful read on what we can give to others.

Greg Levoy, *Callings: Finding and Following an Authentic Life* (Harmony, 1997). If you have any questions as to what you need to do before or after retirement, read this book cover to cover.

Rolling Thunder Speaks: A Message for Turtle Island, ed. Carmen Sun Rising Pope (Clear Light, 1999), p. 193. A collection of interviews with the medicine man, sage, and activist.

Thomas Merton, *The Ascent to Truth* (Viking, 1959), p. 177. Collected commentaries by the Catholic monk and philosopher.

STEP 10

Annie Dillard, *Pilgrim at Tinker Creek* (Harper Magazine Press, 1974), p. 9. A classic on nature, personal introspection, and living your own life.

Joe Dominguez and Vicki Robin, *Your Money or Your Life: Transforming Your Relationship with Money and Achieving Financial Independence* (Penguin, 1992). The bible of financial simplicity, based on a program to determine your life-energy and what working really costs. The first half is classic; the second half not realistic on the investing advice (see my steps 3 through 8).

Vance Packard, *The Waste Makers* (Pocket, 1963). Although dated, this book is still a must-read on our throwaway society.

Philip Slater, *The Pursuit of Loneliness: American Culture at the Breaking Point* (Beacon, 1970), p. 170. Written during the Vietnam era, this is one of the most powerful critiques of American culture ever written.

Carolyn Merchant, *The Death of Nature: Women, Ecology, and the Scientific Revolution* (HarperSanFrancisco, 1980), p. 87. A whole new way of seeing history, science, and culture; an essential read for further explorations into personal ecology.

Michael Fogler, *Un-Jobbing: The Adult Liberation Handbook* (Free Choice, 1997), p. 59. A wonderfully empowering way of seeing work and the rest of your life.

Paul Wachtel, *The Poverty of Affluence: A Psychological Portrait of the American Way of Life* (New Society, 1989), p. 39. A compelling work on how our economy undermines our happiness and security.

Andrew Hacket, *Money: Who Has How Much and Why* (Touchstone, 1997). A stunning investigative study of income and demographics. Guess what? Lawyers make a lot more money than doctors, nurses, teachers, and journalists.

Juliet Schor, *The Overspent American: Upscaling, Downshifting, and the New Consumer* (Basic Books, 1998), p. 5. A Harvard professor's incisive take on "we are what we spend."

George Kinder, *The Seven Stages of Money Maturity: Understanding the Spirit and Value of Money in Everyday Life* (Delacorte, 1997), p. 84. Financial planner and philosopher Kinder explores the psychology and spirit of money. The author was featured in my *Late-Start Investor* (Holt, 1999).

Barbara Brandt, *Whole-Life Economics: Revaluing Daily Life* (New Society, 1995), p. 80. A holistic way of looking at the economics of perpetual growth.

Joel and Michelle Levey, *Living in Balance: A Dynamic Approach for Creating Harmony and Wholeness in a Chaotic World* (Conari, 1998). A comprehensive self-help guide on restoring balance to your life as well as a powerful inspiration.

Mark Burch, *Simplicity: Notes, Stories, and Exercises for Developing Unimaginable Wealth* (New Society, 1995), p. 58. One of the most helpful and least pretentious of the "simplicity movement" texts.

Thomas Moore, *Care of the Soul: A Guide for Cultivating Depth and Sacredness in Everyday Life* (HarperCollins, 1992). The Jungian analyst's wide-ranging bestseller on modern spirituality.

Willis Harman, *Global Mind Change: The Promise of the 21st Century* (Berrett-Koehler, 1998), p. 170. A compendium of positive ideas for the future.

RESOURCES

ESSENTIAL GOVERNMENT SITES

Internal Revenue Service (www.ustreas.irs.gov) Tax forms, advice, and lots of tax information.

Library of Congress (thomas.loc.gov) A one-stop site for government information.

Medicare (www.medicare.gov) A dense pack of information on the nation's largest medical program for retirees.

National Association of Securities Dealers (www.nasdr.com) This quasi-government agency partially regulates securities dealers. You can check the background on your broker, learn about securities fraud and warnings from the National Information Center, or obtain basic rules governing stockbrokers.

Pension Benefit and Guaranty Corporation (www.pbgc.gov) The quasi-government agency that insures defined-benefit pension plans. You can locate a "lost" pension if you—or someone you know—had a defined-benefit plan (and were vested in it) and either left the company or the company terminated the plan.

Securities & Exchange Commission (www.sec.gov) The main entry point to the SEC's EDGAR database of filings by public companies. An invaluable resource for stock investors. Also check out www.edgar.stern.nyu.edu/mutual.html for SEC filings by mutual funds.

Social Security Administration (www.ssa.gov) The mother lode for anything to do with Social Security. You can also order the PEBES form that will help you estimate your future Social Security benefits based on your contributions to the system through your FICA tax withholding. Call 800-772-1213 to receive the form by mail.

U.S. Department of Labor (www.dol.gov) A useful starting place for retirement plan rules, tips, and information on health insurance continuation (COBRA).

U.S. Department of the Treasury (www.ustreas.gov) An indispensable source for everything concerning Treasury and savings bonds. Your first stop when buying Treasury securities.

U.S. House of Representatives (www.house.gov) A useful site for member information, committee assignments, and e-mail addresses.

U.S. Senate (www.senate.gov) Senators' Web sites and committee assignments.

PRIVATE ORGANIZATIONS

American Association of Individual Investors (312-280-0170, www.aaii.com) A nonprofit group with excellent retirement research, articles, and journals.

AARP (www.aarp.org) The American Association of Retired Persons' site is loaded with research, activities, and resources. A must-see.

Center for a New American Dream (802-862-6762) A nonprofit group dedicated to promoting the idea that "less is more."

Employee Benefit and Research Institute (www.ebri.org) Everything you could possibly want to know about retirement and benefits research.

Highlands Program (404-872-9974, www.highlandsprogram.com) A national program for persons considering retirement.

Investment Company Institute (www.ici.org) Sponsored by the mutual fund trade association, it provides useful information on mutual funds.

National Association of Enrolled Agents (www.naea.org) The latest tax news and information on income taxes and filing tips.

National Association of Investors Corporation (www.better-investing.org) The master site for anything connected with investment clubs.

National Association of Realtors (www.realtor.com) An excellent source for real estate relocation across the country.

Third Age (www.thirdage.com) Although extremely commercial, a fountain of resources, chat rooms, and e-mail lists for anything to do with retired people.

COMMERCIAL SITES

Although these sites are supported by advertising, they contain a number of useful pieces of information and software. You are under no obligation to purchase their wares, and I don't propose they are better than other options available.

Bank Rate Monitor (www.bankrate.com) A primary source for the best rates on certificates of deposit, credit cards, and mortgages nationwide.

Banxquote (www.banxquote.com) Next to bankrate.com, a prime source for credit and savings rates.

Deloitte & Touche (www.dtonline.com) A handy resource on taxes, financial planning, and retirement issues.

Fidelity Mutual Funds (www.fidelity.com) While this is a big billboard for hundreds of Fidelity products, check out their retirement-planning software.

Finance Center/SmartCalc (www.financenter.com) Easily one of the most practical calculator sites on the Internet. You can estimate everything from car payments to retirement savings.

HSH (www.hsh.com) The best mortgage rates in the United States.

IBC Financial Data (www.ibcdata.com) The first place to check for the best returns on money-market mutual funds and bond funds.

Insurance Corner (www.insurancecorner.com) A master site for information on insurance agents and news.

Insurance Market (www.insuremarket.com) An omnibus site for quoting a number of insurance products.

Invest-o-rama (www.investorama.com) Provides links to more than 2,000 investment-related sites, including investment club information.

Lifenet (www.lifenet.com) Mortgage calculators and worksheets.

Money Central (www.moneycentral.msn.com) Microsoft's master site on all things financial. Check out their college and scholarship search tools and their many calculators.

Morningstar (www.morningstar.net) One of the most engaging and useful sites on the Web, includes profiles of stocks and mutual funds. One of the best features is an online portfolio-monitoring program that will automatically store and update values on all of your stock and bond holdings. Also includes financial news and columns.

Mortgage Maze (www.maze.com) Mortgage qualifying calculator and credit information (order credit reports online)

Nest Egg (www.nestegg.iddis.com) A large site sponsored by *Investment Dealer Digest,* it features mutual funds, stocks, a retirement calculator, and financial news and articles.

Quicken (www.quicken.com) An omnibus site that allows you to track ten portfolios, obtain stock quotes, track the top-performing mutual funds, and much more.

Quote.com (www.quote.com) Electronic mail stock-quote and alert service.

RAM Research (www.ramresearch.com) A primary source to find the best deals on any type of credit card.

Charles Schwab (www.schwab.com) Run by the discount broker, this is an excellent site for portfolio monitoring, research, mutual funds, and hundreds of other features.

Scott Burns (ww.scottburns.com) Some down-to-earth personal finance columns from the syndicated writer.

Strong Funds (www.strong-funds.com) Provides basic investment/retirement information in its education section.

T. Rowe Price (www.troweprice.com) Provides guidance on retirement and college planning.

Vanguard (www.vanguard.com) Check out their retirement center and free software.

INFORMATION SERVICES AND SEARCH ENGINES

These services are pure information retrievers, pulling all sorts of things from cyberspace, phone books, and beyond. Use them for everything from getting insurance quotes to college searches.

AltaVista (www.altavista.digital.com) One of the most comprehensive search engines available.

Dogpile (www.dogpile.com) A multisearch engine that searches many engines at once; spotty but interesting.

Excite (www.excite.com) A search engine hybrid that offers Yellow Page listings, stock quotes, maps, newsgroups, and e-mail look-ups.

Hoover's Online (www.hoovers.com) Company profiles and links to other sites. Also available on America Online.

Infoseek (www.infoseek.com) A diverse hybrid combining indexing, search engines, and other gateways to Yellow Pages and e-mail look-ups. You can also put an Infoseek "button" on your browser to avoid going directly to their Web site.

Looksmart (www.looksmart.com) A combination search engine/index, it features personalized lists of magazines, news services, and local sites.

Lycos (www.lycos.com) Your basic search engine, with some bells and whistles.

Newslink (www.newslink.org) Links to more than 3,000 publication-sponsored sites.

QuikPages (www.quikpage.com) A national directory of business Web sites.

Yahoo (www.yahoo.com) See their excellent financial section.

MEDIA SITES

Although offering limited information, these sites are good places for background information on nearly any financial topic.

Barrons Online (www.barrons.com) The weekly Dow Jones investment magazine features stock and fund information.

Bloomberg Business News (www.bloomberg.com) News on companies and portfolio-management software.

Business Wire (www.businesswire.com) Company press releases and news.

Consumers Digest (www.consumersdigest.com) A good way to check prices on thousands of vehicles, appliances, and other consumer products. Also see the author's "Issues and Investigations" and "Your Money" archives.

CNN (www.cnn.com) Headlines from the Cable News Network and CNN financial news channel, CNNfn, whose site is linked to cnn.com.

Kiplinger's Personal Finance (www.kiplingers.com) Loaded with features and calculators.

MSNBC (www.msnbc.com) Briefs from the cable network's news coverage also includes some NBC News items.

New York Times (www.nytimes.com) Lead stories from the national newspaper. Also on America Online.

Reuters News Service (www.reuters.com) Hot stories from Reuters wire service.

SmartMoney (www.smartmoney.com) One of the best personal finance sites on the Internet.

USA Today (www.usatoday.com) A searchable site loaded with features.

Wall Street Journal (www.wsj.com) An abbreviated version of the financial newspaper. For the full, searchable version, you pay a subscription fee.

Washington Post (www.washingtonpost.com) A generous site that includes archived stories from the Post's fine columnists, including Jane Bryant Quinn. Its most valuable feature, however, is the ability to search the Associated Press news wires.

Worth Magazine (www.worth.com) The Web site is actually better than the magazine, which is owned by Fidelity Investments. Features include "Ask Peter Lynch," message boards, and useful financial links.

MISCELLANEOUS CONSUMER/SHOPPING
(INCLUDES NONPROFIT AND TRADE GROUPS)
These sites will help you save money on any number of consumer products.

Autobytel (www.autobytel.com) Features quotes on car prices and insurance calculators.

Autosite (www.autosite.com) A vehicle pricing and buying service.

Carsmart (www.carsmart.com) Vehicle pricing service with links to dealers and manufacturers featuring invoice prices.

CCSNY (www.ccsny.org/weblinks) Essential links to consumer groups, credit information, and government information.

Consumer World (www.consumerworld.org) If you go no other place on the Web for consumer information, try this site first. Its 1,500 links are incomparable, everything from the best deals in credit cards to a "private eye" section for locating people, products, and information.

Equifax (www.equifax.com) Information on credit reports.

Essential Information (www.essential.org) The master site that will link you to most of the Ralph Nader–founded consumer groups, including the Center for Auto Safety, Center for Insurance Research, Coalition for Consumer Health and Safety, and Public Citizen.

E-Loan (www.e-loan.com) A mortgage rate service.

E-Town (www.e-town.com) Reviews of home electronics products.

Expedia (www.expedia.msn.com) A bountiful travel site that will help you locate cheapest airfares, rental cars, cruise deals, and more.

Experian (www.experian.com) Information from the credit bureau service.

GTE Superpages (www.bigyellow.com) A master site for searches of phone books, Yellow Pages, classified ads, employment ads, and business Web sites.

Kelley Blue Book (www.kbb.com) The premier source for vehicle prices (used and new).

Mutual Fund Education Alliance (www.mfea.com) The mutual fund trade group features a retirement worksheet.

Mutual Funds Interactive (www.fundsinteractive.com) News and discussion on mutual fund topics.

Parent Soup (www.parentsoup.com) Reviews of baby products, videos, and software.

PC World (www.pcworld.com) Reviews of computers and peripherals.

Popular Mechanics (www.popularmechanics.com) Reviews of vehicles and electronics and articles on home-improvement topics.

Product Reviews (www.productreviewnet.com) Reviews of thousands of appliances, vehicles, computers, and health and beauty items.

Retire Early (www.geocities.com/wallstreet/8257) The best resource on the Internet for early retirees.

TRAC (www.trac.org) A nonprofit consumer group that allows you to compare long-distance phone services and save money.

Travelocity (www.travelocity.com) One of the most comprehensive travel sites.

Virtual Relocation (www.virtualrelocation.com) Profiles of 39,700 communities.

Sources for Health Insurance (Before Age 62)
The following organizations offer group health insurance to their members. If you are not a member, you may need to join. If you can't obtain affordable health insurance through your employer, consider these sources:

Aid Association for Lutherans (414-734-5721).

American Apparel Producers Network (404-843-3171, www.usawear.org)

American Association for Consumer Benefits (800-872-8896)

American Association of Retired Persons (AARP, 202-434-2277, www.aarp.org)

Association of Retired Americans (317-571-6888, www.ara-usa.org)

Best Employers Association (714-765-1000, bestplans @bestplans.com)

Catholic Aid Association (612-490-1070)

Catholic Knights of America (314-351-1029, ckoa@aol.com)

International Association of Business (817-465-2933)

Knights of the Golden Eagle (215-348-4436)

National Association of Bar and Tavern Owners (954-776-7017)

National Association of Private Enterprise (800-223-6273)

National Association of the Professions (212-949-5900)

National Business Association (214-458-0900, danridg@m.airmail)

National Business Owners Association (202-737-6501, 703-838-2850)

National Officers Association (703-438-3060, msgmod@aol.com)

North American Equipment Dealers Association (314-821-7220, www.naeda.com)

Pilots International Association (800-328-3323, 612/588-5175)

Professional Secretaries International (816-891-6600, www.gvi.net/psi)

Small Business Service Bureau (508-756-3513)

Support Services Alliance (518-295-7966)

Government Resources
Consumers Guide to Medicare Supplement Insurance (800-942-4242). An excellent primer on Medigap insurance.

Other Sources
Contact your college alumni association, fraternal/benevolent group, professional/trade associations, or state insurance regulator for other sources of health insurance

INDEX

About the Author

JOHN F. WASIK is the author of six other books, including *The Late-Start Investor* (Holt, 1999), *Green Marketing & Management: A Global Perspective* (Blackwell, 1996), and *The Investment Club Book* (Warner, 1995). He is the three-time winner of the Peter Lisagor Award for Consumer Journalism, the American Society on Aging National Media Award, the Donald Robinson Memorial Award for Investigative Journalism, and several other honors. He is special projects editor of *Consumers Digest* magazine and resides in Lake County, Illinois, with his wife, Kathleen, and daughter, Sarah.